To

_____

From

_____

Date

_____

ABOVE ALL ELSE
Directions for life

TEENS

Above all else, guard your heart, for it affects everything you do.
Proverbs 4:23-27 NLT

The quoted ideas expressed in this book (but not scripture verses) are not, in all cases, exact quotations, as some have been edited for clarity and brevity. In all cases, the author has attempted to maintain the speaker's original intent. In some cases, quoted material for this book was obtained from secondary sources, primarily print media. While every effort was made to ensure the accuracy of these sources, the accuracy cannot be guaranteed. For additions, deletions, corrections or clarifications in future editions of this text, please write FAMILY CHRISTIAN PRESS.

Scripture quotations are taken from:

The Holy Bible, King James Version

The Holy Bible, New International Version (NIV) Copyright © 1973, 1978, 1984, by International Bible Society. Used by permission of Zondervan Publishing House. All rights reserved.

The New American Standard Bible®, (NASB) Copyright © 1960, 1962, 1963, 1968, 1971, 1972, 1973, 1975, 1977, 1995 by The Lockman Foundation. Used by permission.

The Holy Bible, New King James Version (NKJV) Copyright © 1982 by Thomas Nelson, Inc. Used by permission.

The Holy Bible, New Living Translation, (NLT) Copyright © 1996. Used by permission of Tyndale House Publishers, Inc., Wheaton, Illinois 60189. All rights reserved.

New Century Version®. (NCV) Copyright © 1987, 1988, 1991 by Word Publishing, a division of Thomas Nelson, Inc. All rights reserved. Used by permission.

The Holy Bible: Revised Standard Version (RSV). Copyright 1946, 1952, 1959, 1973 by the Division of Christian Education of the National Council of the Churches of Christ in the United States of America. All rights reserved. Used by permission.

The Holy Bible, The Living Bible (TLB), Copyright © 1971 owned by assignment by Illinois Regional Bank N.A. (as trustee). Used by permission of Tyndale House Publishers, Inc., Wheaton, Illinois 60189. All rights reserved.

The Message (MSG) This edition issued by contractual arrangement with NavPress, a division of The Navigators, U.S.A. Originally published by NavPress in English as THE MESSAGE: The Bible in Contemporary Language copyright 2002-2003 by Eugene Peterson. All rights reserved.

The Holman Christian Standard Bible™ (HOLMAN CSB) Copyright © 1999, 2000, 2001 by Holman Bible Publishers. Used by permission.

Cover Design by Kim Russell / Wahoo Designs
Page Layout by Bart Dawson

ISBN 1-58334-368-7
ISBN-13 978-1-58334-368-5

ABOVE ALL ELSE
Directions for life

TEENS

Above all else, guard your heart, for it affects everything you do.

Proverbs 4:23-27 NLT

TABLE OF CONTENTS

Above all else, guard your heart, for it affects everything you do. Avoid all perverse talk; stay far from corrupt speech. Look straight ahead, and fix your eyes on what lies before you. Mark out a straight path for your feet; then stick to the path and stay safe. Don't get sidetracked; keep your feet from following evil.

Proverbs 4:23-27 NLT

ABOVE ALL ELSE . . .

A PARABLE BY TIM WAY

To the casual observer, the old man might have appeared to be dead. He had sat slumped in the large chair for the past three hours—his chin resting on his chest, eyes closed. Every now and then, his eyelids would twitch, or a soft sigh would escape his throat, but other than that, he was perfectly still. An undignified stream of drool had slowly rolled from one corner of his mouth and run into his white beard.

King Solomon was asleep.

The harsh sound of pottery smashing against a wall suddenly interrupted his peace. It was not close, mind you, but close enough to filter into his subconscious and bring him into that foggy place between sleep and wakefulness. For several minutes, he drifted back and forth.

When he'd earlier let weariness overtake him, it was just after noon. Now through half-closed eyelids, he could see that the late afternoon sun pierced through the western windows of the large study at a sharp angle, sending shafts of light through the latticework in the two narrow openings. The brightness made bold geometric patterns on the floor. He sat for some time contemplating the flecks of dust floating in the hazy glow, watching the patterns of light in their almost imperceptible march across the room.

He raised his head. "I love this place," he thought as he looked around. Of all the private rooms in his palace, this study was his favorite—a place he visited often. Now in the later part of his reign, he came here almost daily. Some days he came to escape the grueling pace of palace life, some days to write, and some days just to think or take a nap. Most would consider this sitting and watching and thinking a waste of time, but he did not. Sitting, watching, and thinking had been the genesis of numerous revelations.

"What woke me?" he muttered. "No, not you," he said as he looked down at the large, sleeping dog whose gray muzzle rested on his feet. No one else in his kingdom dared assume such an intimate closeness. "You're almost as ancient as me, old girl," the old king chuckled as he reached to scratch the dog's shaggy head.

Then he heard it again—crashing pottery followed by angry voices coming from the women's chambers. He moaned. "Not again. Why can't they get along? I should have stopped with only one. What made me think that seven hundred wives could exist peacefully with each other? They are like the constant dripping of water, wearing me down little by little. And there are hundreds of them, always nagging, whining, shouting and yapping like a bunch of spoiled children from sunup to sundown."

He put his head in his hands and sighed deeply.

While he only kept fifty or so of his most favored wives at the main palace, even that was no guarantee that they would not become violent with each other. Some did not even speak his language, and some he had only seen on their wedding day. Most of them he had married as a part of what he considered the cost of keeping peace with his neighbors. "And they are quite a cost," he thought. "They have cost me peace of mind and a part of my soul." He was so much closer to Yahweh before all of this marrying and accumulation of wealth.

The king's study was a perfect square—the top story of a tower sitting in the middle of the palace wall, extending four stories up from the ground. The tower's western wall formed a part of the outer wall of the palace. There were windows on all sides—two on each wall. The eastern windows overlooked a large courtyard in the interior of the palace. The courtyard, over three hundred square feet, was surrounded on three sides by the palace's interior buildings, and on the west by the outer wall and the tower. The western windows looked out over one of the busiest streets in Jerusalem. Here, people moved about in their daily routines, unaware that they were often being observed by the king. The north and south windows of the tower room looked down each length of the western palace wall. To the south, he could see the walls of the great temple with the Holy Place extending toward the heavens. The walls of the Holy Place were trimmed in pure gold and gleamed in the setting spring sun. Of all his accomplishments, the Temple of Yahweh was his most prized.

Two of his soldiers could be seen moving along the palace wall on patrol. They were dressed in the crisp blue and white dress uniform of the palace guard. Each carried a polished bronze shield that was a replica of the pure gold shields hanging in the great ceremonial hall, and their spears were tipped with genuine silver. His soldiers were not there because of any known threats to the kingdom, but because prudence demanded that they remain on guard. Besides, the palace walls were three stories high and the entire complex stood as a virtual fortress in the middle of one of the most fortified cities in the world.

The study's stone walls were lined with fragrant cedar from Lebanon. Even though the paneling had been installed fifteen years prior, it still had a sweet fragrance that greeted visitors to the room. Tapestries of incomparable value hung over the paneling—gifts from kings in surrounding countries. The furniture was heavy and finely carved, most of it built for appearance rather than comfort. But the chair in which the king sat was designed specifically for his rather stout frame. Its perfect fit and thick padding, along with a built-in footrest made this the perfect place for thinking—and sleeping.

The room was not originally intended to be a private

study. It was actually built as a part of the defensive aspects of the palace, but because of the extended peace, it was not needed for that purpose. So, the king had long ago claimed it as his personal study—a private sanctuary and his place to write letters, proverbs and poetry. The perfect view of the city and the temple, and the solitude it provided, made this simple room the king's most favorite spot on earth.

Solomon sat for another twenty minutes watching the sun's slow march across the stone floor. It was approaching twilight. Reaching for the wine goblet, he snorted in frustration when he found it empty. He was about to ring the bell to summon a servant when he heard voices filtering up from the street below.

"Here they are again," he said to the dog. Grunting loudly, he pulled himself up out of the chair and shuffled across to the window, the dog following closely but lazily at his heels.

Looking down through the ornate lattice work to the street below, he watched a group of young men in their late teens standing together. They were noisy and brash with a cockiness that came from inexperience and youth. Their voices were far too loud, and even though it was early evening, they were well on their way to being drunk. Their bragging about yet unaccomplished exploits only enhanced their foolishness. If they were trying to impress the palace guards looking down from the wall, they were

wasting their time. Real men like his soldiers were only
mildly amused by boys pretending to be men.

He had observed them here before. They frequented
a tavern two streets over, and were just beginning to
discover the joys of wasting their fathers' money on wine
and who knows what all else.

The king shook his head. "If only they realized how
utterly foolish they sound!" He was glad that his son,
Rehoboam, was not a part of this group. "But only because
I won't let him. If I gave him half a chance he would be
down there with them. No, on second thought, he would
be down there leading them in their folly," he thought.

The group began to move up the street to his right.
One young man, however, hung back. "Hey, Judah, are
you coming with us?" they called out to him.

"Uh, no. Not right now. You go on ahead. Maybe I'll
catch up later. The usual place?" Judah replied, glancing
over his shoulder as he spoke.

"Okay. Sure. Your loss!" they shouted back as they
walked away.

"Maybe there is hope for this one," the old king
thought. But then he looked up the street to his left and
saw her. She was slowly pacing back and forth at the head
of the lane. He had seen her before. She was in her late
twenties; the only wife of an old wealthy merchant who
often left Jerusalem to travel to Lebanon and beyond in
search of wares to sell in his shop. She had married him

not for love, but for his money. Now, as she often did when left by herself, she had painted her face and had traded her everyday clothes for a costume more suited to her true nature. Her clothes were clearly intended to attract the men that visited this street in search for a companion for the night—for a price. Here, on the other side of the city from her home, she could pretend to be someone else, luring men into a squalid rented room that she paid for from the profits of her part-time trade.

What motivated her to act like a prostitute? Was it the money? Not likely. Her husband gave her anything she wanted. Was it the excitement or the need to feel desired? No one aside from her and Yahweh would ever know.

The young man had seen this woman standing on this corner before and had determined that he would one day work up enough courage to approach her. For a price, he knew that he could have her for the evening, even though under normal circumstances, she would not give his young face a second glance.

She stood with her hands on her hips, watching him approach. His steps were a little unsteady, betraying his inability to handle his wine. He was trying his best to act nonchalant, but was unsuccessful in the attempt. Glancing nervously this way and that, he was obviously trying to assure that his father or one of his father's associates was not watching. When he was about five feet away from her, she shocked him by running up, boldly taking his face in her hands, and kissing him full on the mouth.

"Stop!" the king cried out. "You fool!" For a moment Judah hesitated. What was that he had just heard? He looked nervously behind him. Seeing no one, he gave his attention back to the woman.

She threw her head back and laughed loudly. "Come with me, my love. I have the makings of a feast—today I made my offerings, my vows are all paid!" The sound of her voice carried from the street up to the tower window.

"This woman is fit only for stoning," the king muttered to himself. "Moses and my father David would not have put up with this foolishness. Why have we gone so far astray from the ancient ways? The very nerve this woman has—to bring the things of God into this sinful act!"

The young man looked frantically around him. He had not expected her to be so bold or so loud. He was beginning to regret his decision. Besides, she did not look as good up close as she did from the other end of the street, and her breath smelled of stale wine.

"So now I've come to find you, hoping to catch sight of your face—and here you are!" she continued loudly.

"You liar!" thought the king. "You would have latched onto the first idiot that came down the street with money in his pocket."

Putting her arms around the young man and pulling him close, she purred, "Come, my love. I've spread fresh, clean sheets on my bed, colorful imported linens. My bed is covered with spices and exotic fragrances. Come! Let's make love all night and spend the night in ecstatic lovemaking! My husband's not home. He's away on business and he won't be back for a month."

With that, she put her arm through the young man's, and steered him down the street like a sheep going to slaughter, laughing loudly as she led him out of sight.

"If her husband finds out who has been sleeping with her while he is gone, he will have one of his servants cut out this young fool's heart and throw it to his dogs," the king thought. He was suddenly overcome with a great sadness—for the young man and for all of the young men in his nation. "Why, oh why, my Lord, do they behave so foolishly? Why do they act in this manner?"

While he hadn't actually expected an answer, one came clearly and immediately. The sudden impact almost drove him to his knees.

"It is because they have such poor example as a king," the Spirit spoke. "It is because the spiritual fervor has left your kingdom and has been replaced by a shallow, token nod to me, Yahweh, in the midst of obscene materialism. I have blessed you, but you have squandered my blessings by forgetting me!"

Solomon slowly sank into the chair at the desk. Holding his head in his hands, he slowly rocked back and forth as he let the words from the Spirit sink deep into his soul. His mind drifted back over the years of his reign. What promise! What blessings! Now, nothing was left but regrets and broken potential. He had more wealth than he could count, yet he was miserable. His people were wandering further and further away from Yahweh. How could so much be right, and yet everything be so wrong? Oh, for the smile of Yahweh once again!

Solomon sighed as he picked up the quill lying on the desk and dipped it in the inkwell. It had been a long time since he had felt the Spirit stirring in him. Years of self indulgence had dulled the moving of Yahweh on his soul, and the occurrences of divine inspiration on his writing had all but stopped. Today, however, was different. The Spirit's moving had started long before dawn and had continued into the noon hour. The words seemed to spill out of him onto the parchment. It was like years ago, when he regularly felt Yahweh's tug on his heart.

He looked at the last words he had written in the hours before his nap. His thoughts were of his son, Rehoboam, the one that would likely inherit the kingdom. "The boy is brash and foolish," he thought. "He speaks without thinking. Without my strong hand on his backside he would be out on the street with those other drunken fools. He listens to no one but the young men that surround him—young pups of privilege who are totally out of touch with the people. How will he govern a people he does not even understand or care about? Oh, if only he were more like his grandfather, David. I fear for the people of Israel when I go to be with my fathers."

Early that morning, Solomon had walked up the flight of stairs to the tower room and sat in this very spot watching the sun rise over the palace buildings. The Spirit had stirred deeply on his soul and he had written, *"The path of the righteous is like the first gleam of dawn, shining ever brighter till the full light of day. But the way of the wicked is like deep darkness; they do not know what makes them stumble."*

His thoughts went back to the young man on the street. "This could apply fully to him," the king thought. "He is stumbling around in the dark and will end up in a hole that will destroy him."

His thoughts went to his own son. As he began to write, he could feel the stirring once again of the Spirit and his pen moved urgently across the parchment.

"My son, pay attention to what I say; listen closely to my words. Do not let them out of your sight, keep them within your heart; for they are life to those who find them and health to a man's whole body."

Where had he gone wrong? What were the early signs that he was going the wrong direction? His heart had once burned hot for Jehovah. He thought back to the dedication of the temple and that awesome time when the presence of God filled the Holy of Holies on that dedication day. What an experience!

Then there was God's promise to bless him when he chose wisdom over riches. And the blessings that had poured in on him were more than he could have ever imagined in his wildest dreams. He had riches, power, wisdom—success at every turn.

But something happened. Maybe it was the great success. Maybe it was the ease with which wealth came his way. Maybe it was the many wives. He could justify them by saying they were necessary to make alliances, but the fact was that Jehovah had said not to take many wives. The end result was that his heart had grown cold—almost dead.

So, he threw himself into every pursuit he could imagine; intellectual pursuits, money, power, science, and building projects. None of them brought any satisfaction. All of it was pure vanity.

He turned his eyes back to the parchment in front of him. The Spirit's warmth washed over his body, and almost as if his hand took on a life of its own, he wrote again.

"Above all else, guard your heart, for it is the wellspring of life."

"That's it!" he almost shouted. "I have let down my guard and deceived my heart."

"What should I have done, my Lord?" he whispered. The Spirit whispered back the answer softly through his soul. Tears began to course down his wrinkled face, as his quill touched the paper once again.

"Put away perversity from your mouth; keep corrupt talk far from your lips. Let your eyes look straight ahead, fix your gaze directly before you. Make level paths for your feet and take only ways that are firm. Do not swerve to the right or the left; keep your foot from evil."

Through his tears, the old king looked at what he had just written. "My God, I repent before you," he said as he fell to his old knees and wept. "I will take a spotless lamb to your temple when the sun rises in the morning, and make a proper sacrifice for my sins. Forgive me, Yahweh, for letting down the guard on my heart, for speaking in ways that displease you, for looking and coveting what was not really mine to own, and most of all, for taking paths that were not firm. It is too late for me. I have been a poor example to my sons and my nation. I fear the price they will pay for my sins. Be gracious to them, my God."

The sun had set and darkness had settled over the palace when the old king finally rose slowly and stiffly to his feet. He rang the bell for his servant. He would have something sent up from the kitchen to eat. Something simple.

Even though nothing had really changed, he suddenly felt lighter. Though the urging of the Spirit had lifted, he knew that he had probably just written the most important words of his life. He would give them to his son. Would he listen? Probably not, but he would try anyway.

If not Rehoboam, then perhaps someone else in the future would benefit from the words given to him that day by Jehovah.

My son, pay attention to what I say; listen closely to my
   words.
Do not let them out of your sight, keep them within your heart;
For they are life to those who find them
And health to a man's whole body.
Above all else, guard your heart, for it is the wellspring of life.
Put away perversity from your mouth; keep corrupt talk far
   from your lips.
Let your eyes look straight ahead, fix your gaze directly before
   you.
Make level paths for your feet and take only ways that are
   firm.
Do not swerve to the right or the left; keep your foot from evil.

Proverbs 4:20–27

While the scene of the young man and the prostitute is fictional, it has basis in fact and can be found in Proverbs 7:6–23.

INTRODUCTION

The Bible makes it clear: we should guard our hearts "above all else," yet we live in world that encourages us to do otherwise. Here in the 21st century, temptations and distractions are woven into the fabric of everyday life. As Christians, we must be careful. We must resist temptations and we must avoid those places where we are most easily tempted. This book is intended to help.

In Proverbs 4:23-27, we are instructed to guard our words, our eyes, and our path. This text examines these instructions through a collection of essays, Bible verses, and quotations from noted Christian thinkers.

As a way of introducing these ideas, this book began with a parable by Tim Way—a story about temptation in the ancient city of Jerusalem and about how human waywardness, coupled with divine insight, might have influenced the writings of an aged king. Tim's story is followed by a series of practical lessons, lessons about protecting ourselves against the trials and temptations that have become inescapable elements of modern-day life.

Each day, you must make countless choices that can bring you closer to God, or not. When you guard your heart—and when you live in accordance with God's commandments—you will inevitably earn His blessings. But if you make unwise choices—or if you give in to the temptations that surround you—trouble is just around the corner.

Would you like to experience God's peace and His abundance? Then guard your heart above all else. When you're tempted to speak an unkind word, hold your tongue. When you're faced with a difficult choice or a powerful temptation, talk things over with God. When you're uncertain of your next step, follow in the footsteps of Jesus. Invite God into your heart and live according to His commandments. When you do, you will be blessed today, tomorrow, and forever.

PART 1

GUARD
YOUR WORDS

Avoid all perverse talk;
stay far from corrupt speech.

Proverbs 4:24 NLT

GUARD
YOUR SPEECH

Avoid all perverse talk; stay far from corrupt speech.

Proverbs 4:24 NLT

Okay, how can you guard your heart? A great place to start is by guarding your words. And make no mistake—you'll feel better about yourself if you pay careful attention to the things you say.

Of course you must never take the Lord's name in vain, but it doesn't stop there. You must also try to speak words of encouragement, words that lift others up, words that give honor to your Heavenly Father.

When you're frustrated or tired, you may say things that would be better left unsaid. And when you lash out in anger, you will probably miss a wonderful opportunity— the opportunity to consider your thoughts before you speak them.

A far better strategy, of course, is to do the more difficult thing: to think first and to speak next. When you do, you give yourself more time to compose your thoughts and to consult your Creator (but not necessarily in that order!).

The Bible warns that you will be judged by the words you speak (Matthew 12:36-37). And Ephesians 4:29 instructs you to make "each word a gift" (MSG). These passages make it clear that God cares very much about the things you say and the way you say them. And if God cares that much, so should you.

Watch the way you talk.
Let nothing foul or dirty come out of your mouth.
Say only what helps, each word a gift.

Ephesians 4:29 MSG

A TIP FOR GUARDING YOUR HEART

If you're not sure that it's the right thing to say, don't say it! And if you're not sure that it's the truth, don't tell it.

WORDS OF WISDOM

Every word we speak, every action we take, has an effect on the totality of humanity. No one can escape that privilege—or that responsibility.

Laurie Beth Jones

Attitude and the spirit in which we communicate are as important as the words we say.

Charles Stanley

The battle of the tongue is won not in the mouth, but in the heart.

Annie Chapman

The things that we feel most deeply we ought to learn to be silent about, at least until we have talked them over thoroughly with God.

Elisabeth Elliot

A little kindly advice is better than a great deal of scolding.

Fanny Crosby

GOD'S WORDS OF WISDOM

So then, rid yourselves of all evil, all lying, hypocrisy, jealousy, and evil speech. As newborn babies want milk, you should want the pure and simple teaching. By it you can grow up and be saved.

1 Peter 2:1–2 NCV

Be gracious in your speech. The goal is to bring out the best in others in a conversation, not put them down, not cut them out.

Colossians 4:6 MSG

To everything there is a season . . . a time to keep silence, and a time to speak.

Ecclesiastes 3:1,7 KJV

If anyone considers himself religious and yet does not keep a tight rein on his tongue, he deceives himself and his religion is worthless.

James 1:26 NIV

SUMMING IT UP

God understands the importance of the words you speak . . . and so should you.

GUARD YOUR WORDS AGAINST ANGER

Bad temper is contagious—don't get infected.

Proverbs 22:25 MSG

Your temper is either your master or your servant. Either you control it, or it controls you. And the extent to which you allow anger to rule your life will determine, to a surprising degree, the quality of your relationships with others and your relationship with God.

Temper tantrums are usually unproductive, unattractive, unforgettable, and unnecessary. Perhaps that's why Proverbs 16:32 states that, "Controlling your temper is better than capturing a city" (NCV).

If you've allowed anger to become a regular visitor at your house, you should pray for wisdom, for patience, and for a heart that is so filled with forgiveness that it contains no room for bitterness. God will help you terminate your tantrums if you ask Him to—and that's a good thing because anger and peace cannot coexist in the same mind.

If you permit yourself to throw too many tantrums, you will forfeit—at least for now—the peace that might otherwise be yours through Christ. So obey God's Word by turning away from anger today and every day. You'll be glad you did, and so will your family and friends.

> *Don't become angry quickly,*
> *because getting angry is foolish.*
>
> Ecclesiastes 7:9 NCV

A TIP FOR GUARDING YOUR HEART

Mood Adjustment 101: Okay, if you find yourself in a seriously bad mood, there's nothing you can do, right? Wrong! You can always make a mood adjustment. So don't make yourself (and everybody else) miserable. Instead of working yourself up into a frenzy, slow yourself down and redirect your thoughts to things positive, and prayerfully ask God to help you calm down and lighten up. When you ask, He answers.

WORDS OF WISDOM

Anger is the noise of the soul; the unseen irritant of the heart; the relentless invader of silence.

Max Lucado

Acrid bitterness inevitably seeps into the lives of people who harbor grudges and suppress anger, and bitterness is always a poison.

Lee Strobel

When something robs you of your peace of mind, ask yourself if it is worth the energy you are expending on it. If not, then put it out of your mind in an act of discipline. Every time the thought of "it" returns, refuse it.

Kay Arthur

The only justifiable anger defends the great, glorious, and holy nature of our God.

John MacArthur

When you strike out in anger, you may miss the other person, but you will always hit yourself.

Jim Gallery

GOD'S WORDS OF WISDOM

Everyone should be quick to listen, slow to speak and slow to become angry, for man's anger does not bring about the righteous life that God desires.

James 1:19-20 NIV

But I tell you that men will have to give account on the day of judgment for every careless word they have spoken. For by your words you will be acquitted, and by your words you will be condemned.

Matthew 12:36-37 NIV

When you are angry, do not sin, and be sure to stop being angry before the end of the day. Do not give the devil a way to defeat you.

Ephesians 4:26–27 NCV

SUMMING IT UP

Angry words are dangerous to your emotional and spiritual health. So treat anger as an uninvited guest, and usher it away as quickly—and as quietly—as possible.

GUARD YOUR WORDS BY BEING KIND

Kind people do themselves a favor,
but cruel people bring trouble on themselves.

Proverbs 11:17 NCV

Kindness is a choice. Sometimes, when we feel happy or generous, we find it easy to be kind. Other times, when we are discouraged or tired, we can scarcely summon the energy to utter a single kind word. But, God's commandment is clear: He intends that we make the conscious choice to treat others with kindness and respect, no matter our circumstances, no matter our emotions.

In the busyness and confusion of daily life, it is easy to lose focus, and it is easy to become frustrated. We are imperfect human beings struggling to manage our lives as best we can, but we often fall short. When we are distracted or disappointed, we may neglect to share a kind word or a kind deed. This oversight hurts others, but it hurts us most of all.

Today, guard your words carefully—and slow yourself down. Slow down long enough to look for people who need your smile, your kind words, or your helping hand. Make kindness a centerpiece of your dealings with others. They will be blessed, and you will be, too.

Be ye therefore merciful,
as your Father also is merciful.

Luke 6:36 KJV

A TIP FOR GUARDING YOUR HEART

The Golden Rule starts with you, so when in doubt, be a little kinder than necessary.

WORDS OF WISDOM

Kindness in this world will do much to help others, not only to come into the light, but also to grow in grace day by day.

Fanny Crosby

When you launch an act of kindness out into the crosswinds of life, it will blow kindness back to you.

Dennis Swanberg

It is one of the most beautiful compensations of life that no one can sincerely try to help another without helping herself.

Barbara Johnson

Be so preoccupied with good will that you haven't room for ill will.

E. Stanley Jones

When you extend hospitality to others, you're not trying to impress people, you're trying to reflect God to them.

Max Lucado

GOD'S WORDS OF WISDOM

Show respect for all people. Love the brothers and sisters of God's family.

1 Peter 2:17 NCV

May the Lord cause you to increase and abound in love for one another, and for all people.

1 Thessalonians 3:12 NASB

And be ye kind one to another, tenderhearted, forgiving one another, even as God for Christ's sake hath forgiven you.

Ephesians 4:32 KJV

Verily I say unto you, Inasmuch as ye have done it unto one of the least of these my brethren, ye have done it unto me.

Matthew 25:40 KJV

SUMMING IT UP

Kind words have echoes that last a lifetime and beyond.

GUARD YOUR WORDS BY CELEBRATING LIFE

This is the day the LORD has made;
we will rejoice and be glad in it.

Psalm 118:24 NKJV

nother way to guard your words is by making sure that you take time to celebrate life. When you make each day a celebration, you'll be doing yourself and your friends a big-time favor. And, you'll be drawing closer to your Creator.

Are you living the triumphant life that God has promised? Or are you, instead, a spiritual shrinking violet? As you ponder that question, consider this: God does not intend that you live a life that is commonplace or mediocre. And He doesn't want you hide your light "under a basket." Instead, He wants you to "Let your light so shine before men, that they may see your good works and glorify your Father in heaven" (Matthew 5:16 NKJV). In short, God wants you to live a triumphant life so that others might know precisely what it means to be a believer.

The Christian life should be a triumphal celebration, a daily exercise in thanksgiving and praise. Join that celebration today. And while you're at it, make sure that you let everybody—especially friends and family members—know that you've joined.

Delight thyself also in the LORD;
and he shall give thee the desires of thine heart.

Psalm 37:4 KJV

A TIP FOR GUARDING YOUR HEART

Today is a cause for celebration: Psalm 118: 24 has clear instructions for the coming day: "This is the day which the LORD has made; let us rejoice and be glad in it." Plan your day—and your life—accordingly.

WORDS OF WISDOM

If you can forgive the person you were, accept the person you are, and believe in the person you will become, you are headed for joy. So celebrate your life.

Barbara Johnson

Some of us seem so anxious about avoiding hell that we forget to celebrate our journey toward heaven.

Philip Yancey

Life is a glorious opportunity.

Billy Graham

The happiest people in the world are not those who have no problems, but the people who have learned to live with those things that are less than perfect.

James Dobson

Christ is the secret, the source, the substance, the center, and the circumference of all true and lasting gladness.

Mrs. Charles E. Cowman

GOD'S WORDS OF WISDOM

David and the whole house of Israel were celebrating with all their might before the LORD, with songs and with harps, lyres, tambourines, sistrums and cymbals.

2 Samuel 6:5 NIV

At the dedication of the wall of Jerusalem, the Levites were sought out from where they lived and were brought to Jerusalem to celebrate joyfully the dedication with songs of thanksgiving and with the music of cymbals, harps and lyres.

Nehemiah 12:27 NIV

So now we can rejoice in our wonderful new relationship with God—all because of what our Lord Jesus Christ has done for us in making us friends of God.

Romans 5:11 NLT

SUMMING IT UP

God has given you the gift of life (here on earth) and the promise of eternal life (in heaven). Now, He wants you to celebrate those gifts.

GUARD YOUR WORDS WITH INTEGRITY

The integrity of the upright will guide them.

Proverbs 11:3 NKJV

I t has been said that character is what we are when nobody is watching. How true. But there's never really a time when nobody is watching because God is always around, and He's always paying attention. As Bill Hybels observed, "Every secret act of character, conviction, and courage has been observed in living color by our omniscient God." Yep, God sees all; He knows all—and all of us should behave accordingly.

Are you willing to guard your words and watch your steps? If so, you'll discover that living a life of integrity isn't always the easiest way, but it is always the right way.

So if you find yourself tempted to break the truth—or even to bend it—remember that honesty is God's policy . . . and it must also be yours. Simply put, if you really want to walk with God—and if you really want to guard your heart against the dangers of sin—you must protect

your integrity even more carefully than you guard your
wallet. When you do, your character will take care of itself
. . . and you won't need to look over your shoulder to see
who, besides God, is watching.

*A good name is more desirable
than great riches;
to be esteemed is better than silver or gold.*

Proverbs 22:1 NIV

A TIP FOR GUARDING YOUR HEART

Remember: Character is more important than
popularity.

WORDS OF WISDOM

Maintaining your integrity in a world of sham is no small accomplishment.

Wayne Oates

In matters of style, swim with the current. In matters of principle, stand like a rock.

Thomas Jefferson

Character is both developed and revealed by tests, and all of life is a test.

Rick Warren

Each one of us is God's special work of art. Through us, He teaches and inspires, delights and encourages, informs and uplifts all those who view our lives. God, the master artist, is most concerned about expressing Himself—His thoughts and His intentions—through what He paints in our characters.

Joni Eareckson Tada

Image is what people think we are; integrity is what we really are.

John Maxwell

GOD'S WORDS OF WISDOM

Do not be misled: "Bad company corrupts good character."

1 Corinthians 15:33 NIV

Applying all diligence, in your faith supply moral excellence.

2 Peter 1:5 NASB

The righteousness of the blameless clears his path, but the wicked person will fall because of his wickedness.

Proverbs 11:5 Holman CSB

We also have joy with our troubles, because we know that these troubles produce patience. And patience produces character, and character produces hope.

Romans 5:3-4 NCV

SUMMING IT UP

When you tell the truth and do what you know is right, you've got nothing to fear. So you should guard your integrity even more carefully than you guard your wallet.

Guard Your Words by Encouraging Others

When you talk, do not say harmful things,
but say what people need—words that will help others
become stronger. Then what you say will do good
to those who listen to you.

Ephesians 4:29 NCV

I f you want to guard your words, a great way to do it is to be sure that you're constantly spreading encouragement wherever you go. And if you'd like to build a positive self-image, hang out with friends who see the world—and you—in a positive light. When you do, you'll discover that good thoughts are contagious and that you can catch them from your friends.

As Christians, we have every reason to be optimistic about life. As John Calvin observed, "There is not one blade of grass, there is no color in this world that is not intended to make us rejoice." But, sometimes, rejoicing may be the last thing on our minds. Sometimes, we fall prey to worry, frustration, anxiety, or sheer exhaustion. And if we're not careful, we'll spread our pessimism to the people we love most. But God's Word instructs us to do otherwise.

In Ephesians, Paul advises us to speak "words that will help others become stronger." Paul's words still apply.

Your friends and family members probably need more encouragement and less criticism. The same can be said for you. So be a booster, not a cynic—and find friends who do likewise.

Carry one another's burdens;
in this way you will fulfill the law of Christ.

Galatians 6:2 Holman CSB

A TIP FOR GUARDING YOUR HEART

Think carefully about the things you say so that your words can be a "gift of encouragement" to others.

WORDS OF WISDOM

Always stay connected to people and seek out things that bring you joy. Dream with abandon. Pray confidently.

Barbara Johnson

The glory of friendship is not the outstretched hand, or the kindly smile, or the joy of companionship. It is the spiritual inspiration that comes to one when he discovers that someone else believes in him and is willing to trust him with his friendship.

Corrie ten Boom

You can't light another's path without casting light on your own.

John Maxwell

If I am asked how we are to get rid of discouragements, I can only say, as I have had to say of so many other wrong spiritual habits, we must give them up. It is never worth while to argue against discouragement. There is only one argument that can meet it, and that is the argument of God.

Hannah Whitall Smith

GOD'S WORDS OF WISDOM

*Let's see how inventive we can be in encouraging love and
helping out, not avoiding worshipping together as some do but
spurring each other on.*

Hebrews 10:24-25 MSG

*Let the word of Christ dwell in you richly in all wisdom;
teaching and admonishing one another in psalms and hymns
and spiritual songs, singing with grace in your hearts to the
Lord.*

Colossians 3:16 KJV

*But encourage one another day after day, as long as it is still
called "Today," so that none of you will be hardened by the
deceitfulness of sin.*

Hebrews 3:13 NASB

SUMMING IT UP

God's Word encourages you to encourage others.
Enough said.

GUARD YOUR WORDS BY BECOMING A MORE PATIENT PERSON

Always be humble, gentle, and patient,
accepting each other in love.

Ephesians 4:2 NCV

I f you've acquired the unfortunate habit of blurting out the first words that come into your head, perhaps you could use a refresher course in patience. If so, you're not alone. Plenty of people put their mouths in gear before they engage their brains. But God has other plans. God commands us to weigh our words carefully before we speak them (not after!), and He rewards us when we do.

The Bible teaches us to be patient in all things. We must be patient with our brothers and sisters, with our friends, with our parents, with our teachers, with our coaches, and even with casual acquaintances. We are also instructed to be patient with our Heavenly Father as He unfolds His plan for our lives. And that's as it should be. After all, think how patient God has been with us.

But if we look forward to something
we don't have yet,
we must wait patiently and confidently.

Romans 8:25 NLT

A TIP FOR GUARDING YOUR HEART

Take a deep breath, a very deep breath: if you think you're about to say or do something you'll regret later, slow down and take a deep breath, or two deep breaths, or ten, or . . . well you get the idea.

WORDS OF WISDOM

Waiting is an essential part of spiritual discipline. It can be the ultimate test of faith.

Anne Graham Lotz

He knows when we are spiritually ready to receive His blessings to our profit and His glory. Waiting in the sunshine of His love is what will ripen the soul. Be assured that if God waits longer than you could wish, it is only to make the blessing doubly precious. God waited four thousand years, till the fullness of time, before He sent His Son. Our times are in His hands; He will not delay one hour too long.

Andrew Murray

Those who have had to wait and work for happiness seem to enjoy it more, because they never take it for granted.

Barbara Johnson

If you want to hear God's voice clearly and you are uncertain, then remain in His presence until He changes that uncertainty. Often much can happen during this waiting for the Lord. Sometimes He changes pride into humility; doubt into faith and peace . . . .

Corrie ten Boom

GOD'S WORDS OF WISDOM

Patience is better than strength.

Proverbs 16:32 NCV

Patience and encouragement come from God. And I pray that God will help you all agree with each other the way Christ Jesus wants.

Romans 15:5 NCV

The Lord is wonderfully good to those who wait for him and seek him. So it is good to wait quietly for salvation from the Lord.

Lamentations 3:25-26 NLT

Wait on the LORD; Be of good courage, and He shall strengthen your heart; Wait, I say, on the LORD!

Psalm 27:14 NKJV

SUMMING IT UP

Patience pays. Impatience costs.

GUARD YOUR WORDS WITH PRAISE FOR THE CREATOR

Praise the Lord! Oh, give thanks to the Lord, for He is good!
For His mercy endures forever.

Psalm 106:1 NKJV

If you're like most folks on the planet, you're busy . . . very busy. At times, you may feel like there simply aren't enough hours in the day to get everything done. And when the demands of life leave you rushing from place to place with scarcely a moment to spare, you may not take time to praise your Creator. But if you forget to praise God—if you forget to praise Him for who He is and what He's done for you—you're making a big mistake.

The Bible makes it clear: it pays to praise God. In fact, worship and praise should be a part of everything you do. Otherwise, you quickly lose perspective as you fall prey to the demands of everyday life.

Do you really want to know God in a more meaningful way? Then praise Him. And please don't wait until Sunday morning—praise Him all day long, every day, for as long as you live . . . and then for all eternity.

I will praise the Lord at all times,
I will constantly speak his praises.

Psalm 34:1 NLT

A Tip for Guarding Your Heart

All of your talents and abilities come from God. Give Him thanks, and give Him the Glory.

WORDS OF WISDOM

Praise and thank God for who He is and for what He has done for you.

Billy Graham

The joy of the Holy Spirit is experienced by giving thanks in all situations.

Bill Bright

It is always possible to be thankful for what is given rather than to complain about what is not given. One or the other becomes a habit of life.

Elisabeth Elliot

The act of thanksgiving is a demonstration of the fact that you are going to trust and believe God.

Kay Arthur

God is worthy of our praise and is pleased when we come before Him with thanksgiving.

Shirley Dobson

GOD'S WORDS OF WISDOM

Praise him, all you people of the earth, for he loves us with unfailing love; the faithfulness of the Lord endures forever. Praise the Lord!

Psalm 117 NLT

Through Him then, let us continually offer up a sacrifice of praise to God, that is, the fruit of lips that give thanks to His name.

Hebrews 13:15 NASB

Is anyone happy? Let him sing songs of praise.

James 5:13 NIV

It is good to give thanks to the Lord, to sing praises to the Most High. It is good to proclaim your unfailing love in the morning, your faithfulness in the evening.

Psalm 92:1-2 NLT

SUMMING IT UP

God deserves your praise . . . and you deserve the experience of praising Him.

GUARD YOUR WORDS
AGAINST PROFANITY

Avoid all perverse talk; stay far from corrupt speech.

Proverbs 4:24 NLT

Modern society seems to have fallen in love with profanity. You hear offensive language everywhere: on the radio, in the movie theater, on television (especially cable TV!), and in most public places. Yep, you can't deny the fact that bad language has infiltrated our culture at almost every level. And that's too bad.

Just because society embraces profanity doesn't mean that you should embrace it, too. In fact, the opposite should be true: the more vulgar the world becomes, the more determined you should be to avoid using profanity. Why? Because God says so, that's why! Throughout the Bible, God gives plenty of warnings about the use of inappropriate language. And if you're wise, you'll take those warnings to heart even if lots of people don't.

So the next time you hear one of your friends saying things that you wouldn't want your grandparents to hear—the sort of things that you wouldn't say in church—make sure that you don't join in. Profane words are against God's rules, and they should be against your rules, too.

Reckless words pierce like a sword,
but the tongue of the wise brings healing.

Proverbs 12:18 NIV

A TIP FOR GUARDING YOUR HEART

If you can't think of something nice to say . . . don't say anything. It's better to say nothing than to hurt someone's feelings.

WORDS OF WISDOM

The battle of the tongue is won not in the mouth, but in the heart.

Annie Chapman

Attitude and the spirit in which we communicate are as important as the words we say.

Charles Stanley

Words. Do you fully understand their power? Can any of us really grasp the mighty force behind the things we say? Do we stop and think before we speak, considering the potency of the words we utter?

Joni Eareckson Tada

Perhaps we have been guilty of speaking against someone and have not realized how it may have hurt them. Then when someone speaks against us, we suddenly realize how deeply such words hurt, and we become sensitive to what we have done.

Theodore Epp

Every word we speak, every action we take, has an effect on the totality of humanity. No one can escape that privilege—or that responsibility.

Laurie Beth Jones

GOD'S WORDS OF WISDOM

To everything there is a season . . . a time to keep silence, and a time to speak.

Ecclesiastes 3:1,7 KJV

For out of the overflow of the heart the mouth speaks.

Matthew 12:34 NIV

But I say unto you, That every idle word that men shall speak, they shall give account thereof in the day of judgment. For by thy words thou shalt be justified, and by thy words thou shalt be condemned.

Matthew 12:36-37 KJV

Let the words of my mouth, and the meditations of my heart, be acceptable in thy sight, O Lord, my strength and my redeemer.

Psalm 19:14 KJV

SUMMING IT UP

Profanity has absolutely no place in your vocabulary. Period.

PART 2

GUARD
YOUR EYES

Look straight ahead,
and fix your eyes on what lies before you.

Proverbs 4:25 NLT

GUARD YOUR EYES BY CLOSING THEM AT A SENSIBLE HOUR

Come to me, all you who are weary and burdened, and I will give you rest. Take my yoke upon you and learn from me, for I am gentle and humble in heart, and you will find rest for your souls. For my yoke is easy and my burden is light.

Matthew 11:28-30 NIV

A great way to guard your heart and your eyes is by closing your eyelids at a reasonable hour each night. But the world will try to convince you to do otherwise. You live in a world that tempts you to stay up late—very late. But too much late-night TV—or too much late-night partying—is a prescription for exhaustion. And besides, you can get into plenty of trouble in the wee hours of the morning, so if you're concerned about your safety and your health, it's smart to make a habit of turning in at a sensible hour.

Physical exhaustion is God's way of telling you to slow down. God expects you to work hard, of course, and He wants you to enjoy life. But He also intends for you to rest. And if you fail to get the rest that you need, you'll be doing a big disservice to yourself and your family.

Are your physical or spiritual batteries running low? If so, it's time to turn your thoughts and your prayers to God. And when you're finished, it's probably time to turn off the lights and go to bed!

*I will give you a new heart
and put a new spirit within you.*

Ezekiel 36:26 Holman CSB

A TIP FOR GUARDING YOUR HEART

Get Adequate Rest: Without it, you'll tend to become easily frustrated, anxious, and irritable. Sleep deprivation makes clear thinking difficult; too much sleep deprivation makes clear thinking impossible.

WORDS OF WISDOM

Satan does some of his worst work on exhausted Christians when nerves are frayed and their minds are faint.

Vance Havner

Life is strenuous. See that your clock does not run down.

Mrs. Charles E. Cowman

Prescription for a happier and healthier life: resolve to slow down your pace; learn to say no gracefully; resist the temptation to chase after more pleasure, more hobbies, and more social entanglements.

James Dobson

One reason so much American Christianity is a mile wide and an inch deep is that Christians are simply tired. Sometimes you need to kick back and rest for Jesus' sake.

Dennis Swanberg

Jesus taught us by example to get out of the rat race and recharge our batteries.

Barbara Johnson

GOD'S WORDS OF WISDOM

I said to myself, "Relax and rest. God has showered you with blessings."

Psalm 116:7 MSG

I find rest in God; only he gives me hope.

Psalm 62:5 NCV

Full of hope, you'll relax, confident again; you'll look around, sit back, and take it easy.

Job 11:18 MSG

And the apostles gathered themselves together unto Jesus, and told him all things, both what they had done, and what they had taught. And he said unto them, Come ye yourselves apart into a desert place, and rest a while.

Mark 6:30-31 Holman CSB

SUMMING IT UP

Your body, which is a priceless gift from God, needs a sensible amount of sleep each night. Schedule your life accordingly.

GUARD YOUR EYES AGAINST TEMPTATION

Look straight ahead,
and fix your eyes on what lies before you.

Proverbs 4:25 NLT

If you stop to think about it, the cold, hard evidence is right in front of your eyes: you live in a temptation-filled world. The devil is out on the street, hard at work, causing pain and heartache in more ways than ever before. Yep, you live in a temptation nation, a place where the bad guys are working 24/7 to lead you astray. That's why you must remain vigilant. Not only must you resist Satan when he confronts you, but you must also avoid those places where Satan can most easily tempt you.

In a letter to believers, Peter offers a stern warning: "Your adversary, the devil, prowls around like a roaring lion, seeking someone to devour" (I Peter 5:8 NASB).

What was true in New Testament times is equally true in our own. Satan tempts his prey and then devours them (and it's up to you—and only you—to make sure that you're not one of the ones being devoured!).

As believing Christians, we must beware because temptations are everywhere. Satan is determined to win; we must be equally determined that he does not.

> *Put on the full armor of God*
> *so that you can stand against*
> *the tactics of the Devil.*
>
> *Ephesians 6:11 Holman CSB*

A TIP FOR GUARDING YOUR HEART

You live in a society where temptations are everywhere. Your job is to aggressively avoid those temptations before the devil can get his hooks into you.

WORDS OF WISDOM

Do not fight the temptation in detail. Turn from it. Look ONLY at your Lord. Sing. Read. Work.

Amy Carmichael

Instant intimacy is one of the leading warning signals of a seduction.

Beth Moore

Our Lord has given us an example of how to overcome the devil's temptations. When He was tempted in the wilderness, He defeated Satan every time by the use of the Bible.

Billy Graham

Take a really honest look at yourself. Have any old sins begun to take control again? This would be a wonderful time to allow Him to bring fresh order out of longstanding chaos.

Charles Swindoll

Temptation is not a sin. Even Jesus was tempted. The Lord Jesus gives you the strength needed to resist temptation.

Corrie ten Boom

GOD'S WORDS OF WISDOM

But remember that the temptations that come into your life are no different from what others experience. And God is faithful. He will keep the temptation from becoming so strong that you can't stand up against it. When you are tempted, he will show you a way out so that you will not give in to it.

1 Corinthians 10:13 NLT

My child, if sinners try to lead you into sin, do not follow them.

Proverbs 1:10 NCV

So let God work his will in you. Yell a loud no to the Devil and watch him scamper. Say a quiet yes to God and he'll be there in no time. Quit dabbling in sin. Purify your inner life. Quit playing the field.

James 4:7-8 MSG

SUMMING IT UP

Because you live in a temptation-filled world, you must guard your eyes, your thoughts, and your heart—all day, every day.

GUARD YOUR EYES AGAINST ENVY

*But if you harbor bitter envy and selfish ambition in your
hearts, do not boast about it or deny the truth. Such "wisdom"
does not come down from heaven but is earthly, unspiritual,
of the devil. For where you have envy and selfish ambition,
there you find disorder and every evil practice.*

James 3:14-17 NIV

In a competitive, cut-throat world where almost
everybody seems to be in love with material
possessions, it's easy to become envious of other
people's stuff. But it's wrong. So we must learn to guard
our eyes and our hearts against envy . . . or suffer the
consequences.

God's Word teaches us that envy is inappropriate, but
because we are highly imperfect human beings, we may
still find ourselves struggling with feelings of jealousy,
or resentment, or both. These feelings may be especially
powerful when we watch other people get their hands on
things we wish we had.

Have you recently observed someone else catch a lucky break? Or have you seen somebody work hard to achieve big-time success? And when you saw these things, were you jealous? If so, it's time to correct your spiritual eyesight by focusing more on what God has done for you and less on what He's done for other folks.

So here's a surefire formula for a happier, healthier life: Count your own blessings and let your neighbors count theirs. It's the right way to live.

> *Stop your anger! Turn from your rage!*
> *Do not envy others—it only leads to harm.*
>
> *Psalm 37:8 NLT*

A TIP FOR GUARDING YOUR HEART

You can be envious, or you can be happy, but you can't be both. Envy and happiness can't live at the same time in the same brain.

WORDS OF WISDOM

As a moth gnaws a garment, so does envy consume a man.

St. John Chrysostom

What God asks, does, or requires of others is not my business; it is His.

Kay Arthur

When you envy your neighbor, you give demons a place to rest.

Ephraem the Syrian

Contentment comes when we develop an attitude of gratitude for the important things we do have in our lives that we tend to take for granted if we have our eyes staring longingly at our neighbor's stuff.

Dave Ramsey

When you worry about what you don't have, you won't be able to enjoy what you do have.

Charles Swindoll

GOD'S WORDS OF WISDOM

We must not become conceited, provoking one another, envying one another.

Galatians 5:26 Holman CSB

If your sinful nature controls your mind, there is death. But if the Holy Spirit controls your mind, there is life and peace.

Romans 8:6 NLT

I have told you these things, so that in me you may have peace. In this world you will have trouble. But take heart! I have overcome the world.

John 16:33 NIV

Do not covet your neighbor's house . . . or anything that belongs to your neighbor.

Exodus 20:17 Holman CSB

SUMMING IT UP

Envy is a sin. Plus, it's a major-league waste of time and energy. So get over it.

GUARD YOUR EYES AGAINST MEDIA LIES

Don't become so well-adjusted to your culture that you fit into it without even thinking. Instead, fix your attention on God. You'll be changed from the inside out. Readily recognize what he wants from you, and quickly respond to it. Unlike the culture around you, always dragging you down to its level of immaturity, God brings the best out of you, develops well-formed maturity in you.

Romans 12:2 MSG

Sometimes it's hard being a Christian, especially when the world keeps pumping out messages that are contrary to your faith.

The media is working around the clock in an attempt to rearrange your priorities. The media says that your appearance is all-important, that your clothes are all-important, that your car is all-important, and that partying is all-important. But guess what? Those messages are lies. The important things in your life have little to do with parties or appearances. The all-important things in life have to do with your faith, your family, and your future. Period.

Are you willing to stand up for your faith? If so, you'll be doing yourself a king-sized favor. And consider this: When you begin to speak up for God, isn't it logical to assume that you'll also begin to know Him in a more meaningful way? Of course you will.

So do yourself a favor: forget the media hype, and pay attention to God. Stand up for Him and be counted, not just in church where it's relatively easy to be a Christian, but also outside the church, where it's significantly harder. You owe it God . . . and you owe it to yourself.

A TIP FOR GUARDING YOUR HEART

Don't Trust the Media's Messages: Many of the messages that you receive from the media are specifically designed to sell you products that interfere with your spiritual, physical, or emotional health. God takes great interest in your health; the moguls from Madison Avenue take great interest in your pocketbook. Trust God.

WORDS OF WISDOM

The more we stuff ourselves with material pleasures, the less we seem to appreciate life.

Barbara Johnson

All those who look to draw their satisfaction from the wells of the world—pleasure, popularity, position, possessions, politics, power, prestige, finances, family, friends, fame, fortune, career, children, church, clubs, sports, sex, success, recognition, reputation, religion, education, entertainment, exercise, honors, health, hobbies—will soon be thirsty again!

Anne Graham Lotz

The only ultimate disaster that can befall us, I have come to realize, is to feel ourselves to be home on earth.

Max Lucado

The true Christian, though he is in revolt against the world's efforts to brainwash him, is no mere rebel for rebellion's sake. He dissents from the world because he knows that it cannot make good on its promises.

A. W. Tozer

GOD'S WORDS OF WISDOM

For whatever is born of God overcomes the world. And this is the victory that has overcome the world—our faith.

1 John 5:4 NKJV

Religion that God our Father accepts as pure and faultless is this: to look after orphans and widows in their distress and to keep oneself from being polluted by the world.

James 1:27 NIV

If you lived on the world's terms, the world would love you as one of its own. But since I picked you to live on God's terms and no longer on the world's terms, the world is going to hate you.

John 15:19 MSG

Do not love the world or the things in the world. If you love the world, the love of the Father is not in you.

1 John 2:15 NCV

SUMMING IT UP

The popular media has a way of attacking your senses and your heart. Approach the media with care.

GUARD YOUR EYES AGAINST MATERIALISM

And He told them, "Watch out and be on guard against all greed, because one's life is not in the abundance of his possessions."

Luke 12:15 Holman CSB

I s "shop till you drop" your motto? Hopefully not. On the grand stage of a well-lived life, material possessions should play a rather small role. Of course, we all need the basic necessities of life, but once we meet those needs, the piling up of stuff creates more problems than it solves.

Our society is in love with money and the things that money can buy. God is not. God cares about people, not possessions, and so must we. We must, to the best of our abilities, love our neighbors as ourselves, and we must, to the best of our abilities, resist the mighty temptation to place possessions ahead of people.

How much stuff is too much stuff? Well, if your desire for stuff is getting in the way of your desire to know God, then you've got too much stuff—it's as simple as that.

If you find yourself wrapped up in the concerns of the material world, it's time to reorder your priorities by turning your thoughts to more important matters. And, it's time to begin storing up riches that will endure throughout eternity: the spiritual kind. Money, in and of itself, is not evil; worshipping money is. So today, as you prioritize matters of importance in your life, remember that God is almighty, but the dollar is not.

*For where your treasure is,
there your heart will be also.*

Luke 12:34 NKJV

A TIP FOR GUARDING YOUR HEART

Too Much Stuff: Too much stuff doesn't ensure happiness. In fact, having too much stuff can actually prevent happiness.

WORDS OF WISDOM

The socially prescribed affluent, middle-class lifestyle has become so normative in our churches that we discern little conflict between it and the Christian lifestyle prescribed in the New Testament.

Tony Compolo

A society that pursues pleasure runs the risk of raising expectations ever higher, so that true contentment always lies tantalizingly out of reach.

Philip Yancey and Paul Brand

We are made spiritually lethargic by a steady diet of materialism.

Mary Morrison Suggs

Greed is enslaving. The more you have, the more you want—until eventually avarice consumes you.

Kay Arthur

Here's a simple test: If you can see it, it's not going to last. The things that last are the things you cannot see.

Dennis Swanberg

GOD'S WORDS OF WISDOM

No one can serve two masters. The person will hate one master and love the other, or will follow one master and refuse to follow the other. You cannot serve both God and worldly riches.

Matthew 6:24 NCV

For the mind-set of the flesh is death, but the mind-set of the Spirit is life and peace.

Romans 8:6 Holman CSB

Since we entered the world penniless and will leave it penniless, if we have bread on the table and shoes on our feet, that's enough.

1 Timothy 6:7-8 MSG

He who trusts in his riches will fall, but the righteous will flourish . . . .

Proverbs 11:28 NKJV

SUMMING IT UP

Material possessions may seem important at first, but they're nothing compared to the spiritual rewards that God gives to people (like you) who put Him first.

GUARD YOUR EYES BY REJECTING IMMORALITY

*Honor marriage, and guard the sacredness of sexual intimacy
between wife and husband.
God draws a firm line against casual and illicit sex.*

Hebrews 13:4 MSG

The decision to have sex before you're married—or the decision to abstain from it—is a choice that will most certainly impact the rest of your life. That decision will play an important role in the way you see yourself, and it will play an important role in the way you view relationships with members of the opposite sex. And, of course, there's always the chance that your decision to have sex might result in an unexpected "surprise."

Face it: there's a lot riding on the decision to abstain from sex. And because it's an important decision, you should think about it—and pray about it—before you make a decision that might just change the direction of your life.

Perhaps you have friends who boast about sex. If so, it may seem to you that "everybody is doing it." But they're not. In fact, millions of young adults know that premarital sex is just plain wrong. And you must understand it, too.

When you think about it, the argument in favor of abstinence isn't a very hard case to make. First and foremost, abstinence is a part of God's plan for people who are not married. Period. But it doesn't stop there: abstinence is also the right thing to do and the smart thing to do.

If you're involved with people who try to convince you that it's okay to have sex before marriage, you're hanging out with the wrong people. So do yourself a favor: find friends who know that everybody isn't doing it . . . because they aren't!

A TIP FOR GUARDING YOUR HEART

Sometimes, immorality is obvious and sometimes, it's not. So beware: the most subtle forms of sin are often the most dangerous.

WORDS OF WISDOM

The Bible has a word to describe "safe" sex. It's called marriage.

Gary Smalley & John Trent

But suppose we do sin. Suppose we slip and fall. Suppose we yield to temptation for a moment. What happens? We have to confess that sin.

Billy Graham

Good and evil both increase at compound interest. That is why the little decisions you and I make every day are of such infinite importance.

C. S. Lewis

A healthy fear of God will do much to deter us from sin.

Charles Swindoll

We must recognize that when we face deeply rooted habits of sin in daily spiritual warfare, self-help is no help at all. There is only one cure, and it comes from God.

Jim Cymbala

GOD'S WORDS OF WISDOM

*If we say that we have no sin, we deceive ourselves, and
the truth is not in us. If we confess our sins, He is faithful
and just to forgive us our sins and to cleanse us from all
unrighteousness.*

1 John 1:8-9 NKJV

*All who indulge in a sinful life are dangerously lawless, for sin
is a major disruption of God's order.*

1 John 3:4 MSG

*Since we've compiled this long and sorry record as sinners
(both us and them) and proved that we are utterly incapable of
living the glorious lives God wills for us, God did it for us. Out
of sheer generosity he put us in right standing with himself. A
pure gift. He got us out of the mess we're in and restored us to
where he always wanted us to be. And he did it by means of
Jesus Christ.*

Romans 3:23 MSG

SUMMING IT UP

Your body is a temple, so treat it with respect . . . or
face the consequences.

PART 3

GUARD YOUR STEPS

Mark out a straight path for your feet;
then stick to the path and stay safe.
Don't get sidetracked;
keep your feet from following evil.

Proverbs 4:26-27 NLT

GUARD YOUR STEPS BY MAKING YOUR PATH STRAIGHT

Mark out a straight path for your feet;
then stick to the path and stay safe.

Proverbs 4:26 NLT

Okay, answer this question honestly: Do you behave differently because of your relationship with Jesus? Or do you behave in pretty much the same way that you would if you weren't a believer? Hopefully, you've invited Christ to reign over your heart—and hopefully that means you've made BIG changes in your thoughts and your actions.

The Bible teaches you to follow a "straight path" by obeying God's commandments. But as everybody knows, being obedient isn't always easy, especially when you're living in a culture that glamorizes disobedience. It's hard to stay on the right path when society is leading you down the wrong path, but it's up to you (and only you) to watch your step . . . or else.

If you're determined to follow "the crowd," you may soon find yourself headed in the wrong direction. But if you make up your mind to follow the One from Galilee, you'll be safe now and forever. So here's some advice: Don't follow the crowd—follow Jesus. And keep following Him every day of your life, beginning with this day.

> *In everything set them an example*
> *by doing what is good.*
>
> *Titus 2:7 NIV*

A TIP FOR GUARDING YOUR HEART

Try as we might, we simply cannot escape the consequences of our actions. How we behave today has a direct impact on the rewards we will receive tomorrow. That's a lesson that we must teach our students by our words and our actions, but not necessarily in that order.

WORDS OF WISDOM

Conviction is worthless until it is converted into conduct.

Thomas Carlyle

The purity of motive determines the quality of action.

Oswald Chambers

Although God causes all things to work together for good for His children, He still holds us accountable for our behavior.

Kay Arthur

There may be no trumpet sound or loud applause when we make a right decision, just a calm sense of resolution and peace.

Gloria Gaither

Study the Bible and observe how the persons behaved and how God dealt with them. There is explicit teaching on every condition of life.

Corrie ten Boom

GOD'S WORDS OF WISDOM

*Are there those among you who are truly wise and
understanding? Then they should show it by living right and
doing good things with a gentleness that comes from wisdom.*

James 3:13 NCV

*Even a child is known by his actions, by whether his conduct is
pure and right.*

Proverbs 20:11 NIV

*Here is a simple, rule-of-thumb for behavior: Ask yourself
what you want people to do for you, then grab the initiative
and do it for them. Add up God's Law and Prophets and this is
what you get.*

Matthew 7:12 MSG

*Light shines on the godly, and joy on those who do right. May
all who are godly be happy in the Lord and praise his holy
name.*

Psalm 97:11-12 NLT

SUMMING IT UP

How can you guard your steps? By walking with Jesus
every day of your life.

GUARD YOUR STEPS WITH A DAILY DEVOTIONAL

*Every morning he wakes me. He teaches me to listen
like a student. The Lord God helps me learn . . . .*

Isaiah 50:4-5 NCV

Want to guard your steps and guard your heart? Then schedule a meeting with God every single day.

Daily life is a tapestry of habits, and no habit is more important to your spiritual health than the discipline of daily prayer and devotion to the Creator. When you begin each day with your head bowed and your heart lifted, you are reminded of God's love and God's laws.

Each day has 1,440 minutes—do you value your relationship with God enough to spend a few of those minutes with Him? He deserves that much of your time and more. But if you find that you're simply "too busy" for a daily chat with your Father in heaven, it's time to take a long, hard look at your priorities and your values.

If you've acquired the unfortunate habit of trying to "squeeze" God into the corners of your life, it's time to reshuffle the items on your to-do list by placing God first. God wants your undivided attention, not the leftovers of your day. So, if you haven't already done so, form the habit of spending quality time with your Creator. He deserves it . . . and so, for that matter, do you.

Truly my soul silently waits for God;
from Him comes my salvation.

Psalm 62:1 NKJV

A Tip for Guarding Your Heart

Begin each day with a few minutes of quiet time to organize your thoughts. During this time, read at least one uplifting Bible passage and thus begin your day on a positive, productive note.

WORDS OF WISDOM

We must appropriate the tender mercy of God every day after conversion or problems quickly develop. We need his grace daily in order to live a righteous life.

Jim Cymbala

Make a plan now to keep a daily appointment with God. The enemy is going to tell you to set it aside, but you must carve out the time. If you're too busy to meet with the Lord, friend, then you are simply too busy.

Charles Swindoll

It is necessary to eat every day to maintain strength and energy. When we don't, our bodies weaken. The same is true with our spirits. To maintain spiritual strength, we must feed our spirits every day with the Word of God, our spiritual food.

Cynthia Heald

Our devotion to God is strengthened when we offer Him a fresh commitment each day.

Elizabeth George

Surrender your mind to the Lord at the beginning of each day.

Warren Wiersbe

GOD'S WORDS OF WISDOM

May the words of my mouth and the thoughts of my heart be pleasing to you, O Lord, my rock and my redeemer.

Psalm 19:14 NLT

Be still, and know that I am God.

Psalm 46:10 NKJV

It is good to give thanks to the Lord, to sing praises to the Most High. It is good to proclaim your unfailing love in the morning, your faithfulness in the evening.

Psalm 92:1-2 NLT

But grow in the grace and knowledge of our Lord and Savior Jesus Christ. To Him be the glory both now and to the day of eternity.

2 Peter 3:18 Holman CSB

SUMMING IT UP

You need to talk to your Creator every day. God is ready to talk to you, and you should be ready to talk to Him first thing every morning.

11/16/07

GUARD YOUR STEPS BY MAKING GODLY CHOICES

*If you need wisdom—if you want to know what
God wants you to do—ask him, and he will gladly tell you.
He will not resent your asking.*

James 1:5 NLT

Face facts: your life is a series of choices. From the instant you wake up in the morning until the moment you nod off to sleep at night, you make countless decisions—decisions about the things you do, decisions about the words you speak, and decisions about the way that you choose to direct your thoughts.

As a believer who has been transformed by the love of Jesus Christ, you have every reason to make wise choices. But sometimes, when the daily grind threatens to grind you up and spit you out, you may make choices that are displeasing to God. When you do, you'll pay a price because you'll forfeit the happiness and the peace that might otherwise have been yours.

So, as you pause to consider the kind of Christian you are—and the kind of Christian you want to become—ask yourself whether you're sitting on the fence or standing in the light. And then, if you sincerely want to follow in the footsteps of the One from Galilee, make choices that are pleasing to Him. He deserves no less . . . and neither, for that matter, do you.

A Tip for Guarding Your Heart

First you'll make choices . . . and before you know it, your choices will make you. So take time to think carefully about the direction of your life and the choices that you've been making. Then, try to come up with at least one "new and improved" choice that you can make today.

WORDS OF WISDOM

Every day, I find countless opportunities to decide whether I will obey God and demonstrate my love for Him or try to please myself or the world system. God is waiting for my choices.

Bill Bright

Every time you make a choice, you are turning the central part of you, the part that chooses, into something a little different from what it was before.

C. S. Lewis

Life is pretty much like a cafeteria line—it offers us many choices, both good and bad. The Christian must have a spiritual radar that detects the difference not only between bad and good but also among good, better, and best.

Dennis Swanberg

Choices can change our lives profoundly. The choice to mend a broken relationship, to say "yes" to a difficult assignment, to lay aside some important work to play with a child, to visit some forgotten person—these small choices may affect many lives eternally.

Gloria Gaither

GOD'S WORDS OF WISDOM

I am offering you life or death, blessings or curses. Now, choose life! . . . To choose life is to love the Lord your God, obey him, and stay close to him.

Deuteronomy 30:19-20 NCV

But Daniel purposed in his heart that he would not defile himself . . . .

Daniel 1:8 KJV

The thing you should want most is God's kingdom and doing what God wants. Then all these other things you need will be given to you.

Matthew 6:33 NCV

So I strive always to keep my conscience clear before God and man.

Acts 24:16 NIV

SUMMING IT UP

Every day you make hundreds of choices . . . and the quality of those choices determines the quality of your day and your life.

GUARD YOUR STEPS WITH GODLY FRIENDS

As iron sharpens iron, a friend sharpens a friend.

Proverbs 27:17 NLT

Some friendships help us guard our hearts; these friendships should be nurtured. Other friendships place us in situations where we are tempted to dishonor God by disobeying His commandments; friendships such as these have the potential to do us great harm.

Because we tend to become like our friends, we must choose our friends carefully. Because our friends influence us in ways that are both subtle and powerful, we must ensure that our friendships are pleasing to God. When we spend our days in the presence of godly believers, we are blessed, not only by those friends, but also by our Creator.

Are you hanging out with people who make you a better Christian, or are you spending time with people who encourage you to stray from your faith? The answer to this question will have a surprising impact on the condition of your spiritual health. Why? Because peer pressure is very real and very powerful. So, one of the best ways to ensure that you follow Christ is to find fellow believers who are willing to follow Him with you.

Many elements of society seek to mold you into a more worldly being; God, on the other hand, seeks to mold you into a new being, a new creation through Christ, a being that is most certainly not conformed to this world. If you are to please God, you must resist the pressures that society seeks to impose upon you, and you must choose, instead, to follow in the footsteps of His only begotten Son.

A TIP FOR GUARDING YOUR HEART

Your choice of friends is critically important. If you want to accomplish your highest aspirations, you should choose friends who will encourage you to accomplish those aspirations.

WORDS OF WISDOM

True friendship can harbor no suspicion; a friend must speak to a friend as freely as to his second self.

St. Jerome

Trust is the soil in which the flower of friendship grows.

Marie T. Freeman

Becoming a good friend is aerobic in that it takes time and effort. We don't just wake up one day, and voila: we are Wonder Friend!

Patsy Clairmont

Friendship fills a deep well within me with fresh water. When I celebrate my friendships, it's like dropping a huge rock into the well. It splashes that water everywhere, on everyone else in my life.

Nicole Johnson

Friendship is the greatest of worldly goods. Certainly to me it is the chief happiness of life. If I had to give a piece of advice to a young man about a place to live, I think I should say, "sacrifice almost everything to live where you can be near your friends." I know I am very fortunate in that respect.

C. S. Lewis

GOD'S WORDS OF WISDOM

Beloved, if God so loved us, we also ought to love one another.

1 John 4:11 NKJV

Greater love has no one than this, that he lay down his life for his friends.

John 15:13 NIV

I thank my God upon every remembrance of you.

Philippians 1:3 NKJV

A friend loves at all times, and a brother is born for adversity.

Proverbs 17:17 NIV

If a fellow believer hurts you, go and tell him—work it out between the two of you. If he listens, you've made a friend.

Matthew 18:15 MSG

SUMMING IT UP

Thank God for friends who make you a better person and a better Christian. These friends are gifts from above. Treat them that way.

GUARD YOUR STEPS BY LIVING ACCORDING TO YOUR BELIEFS

But prove yourselves doers of the word,
and not merely hearers.

James 1:22 NASB

This world is inhabited by quite a few people who are very determined to do bad things. The devil and his human helpers are working around the clock to cause pain and heartbreak in every corner of the globe . . . including your corner. So you'd better beware.

Your job, if you choose to accept it, is to recognize bad behavior and fight it. How? By standing up for your beliefs, that's how!

The moment that you decide to fight evil whenever you see it—the moment you decide to stand up for the

One who gave His life for you—you can no longer be a lukewarm, halfhearted Christian. And, when you are no longer a lukewarm Christian, God rejoices (and the devil doesn't).

So when in doubt, stand up for your beliefs. And don't just stand over there in the corner with your shoulders slumped and your head hanging low; stand up straight, hold your head high, and be counted—proudly—for Jesus. Remember that in the battle of good versus evil, the devil never takes a day off . . . and neither should you.

A TIP FOR GUARDING YOUR HEART

Why is it so much easier to talk about being a good person than it is to actually be one? Face it: talking about your beliefs is easy. But, making your actions match your words is much harder! Why? Because you are a normal human being, and that means that you can be tempted by stuff and by people. Nevertheless, if you really want to be honest with yourself, then you must make your actions match your beliefs. Period.

WORDS OF WISDOM

The mind is a faculty, and a magnificent one at that. But the heart is the dwelling place of our true beliefs.

John Eldredge

What we believe determines how we behave, and both determine what we become.

Warren Wiersbe

As the body lives by breathing, so the soul lives by believing.

Thomas Brooks

Belief is not the result of an intellectual act; it is the result of an act of my will whereby I deliberately commit myself.

Oswald Chambers

Believe and do what God says. The life-changing consequences will be limitless, and the results will be confidence and peace of mind.

Franklin Graham

GOD'S WORDS OF WISDOM

You never saw him, yet you love him. You still don't see him, yet you trust him—with laughter and singing. Because you kept on believing, you'll get what you're looking forward to: total salvation.

1 Peter 1:8-9 MSG

I know whom I have believed and am persuaded that He is able to guard what has been entrusted to me until that day.

2 Timothy 1:12 Holman CSB

Again, this is God's command: to believe in his personally named Son, Jesus Christ. He told us to love each other, in line with the original command. As we keep his commands, we live deeply and surely in him, and he lives in us. And this is how we experience his deep and abiding presence in us: by the Spirit he gave us.

1 John 3:23-24 MSG

SUMMING IT UP

When you live in sync with your beliefs, God will guide your steps and protect your heart.

Guard Your Steps by Leading a Disciplined Lifestyle

Discipline yourself for the purpose of godliness.

1 Timothy 4:7 NASB

Are you a self-disciplined person? If so, congratulations . . . if not, God wants to have a little talk with you.

God doesn't reward laziness, misbehavior, or apathy. To the contrary, He expects His followers to behave with dignity and discipline. But sometimes, it's extremely difficult to be dignified and disciplined. Why? Because the world wants us to believe that dignified, self-disciplined behavior is going out of style.

You live in a world in which leisure is glorified and indifference is often glamorized. But God has other plans.

He did not create you to be ordinary; He created you for far greater things.

Face facts: Life's greatest rewards aren't likely to fall into your lap. To the contrary, your greatest accomplishments will probably require lots of work, which is perfectly fine with God. After all, He knows that you're up to the task, and He has big plans for you. God will do His part to fulfill those plans, and the rest, of course, is up to you.

Now, are you steadfast in your determination to be a self-disciplined person? If so, give yourself a pat on the back . . . if not, reread this little essay—and keep reading it—until God's message finally sinks in.

A TIP FOR GUARDING YOUR HEART

A disciplined lifestyle gives you more control: The more disciplined you become, the more you can take control over your life (which, by the way, is far better than letting your life take control over you).

WORDS OF WISDOM

Man's great danger is the combination of his increased control over the elements and his lack of control over himself.

Albert Schweitzer

Work is doing it. Discipline is doing it every day. Diligence is doing it well every day.

Dave Ramsey

As we seek to become disciples of Jesus Christ, we should never forget that the word disciple is directly related to the word discipline. To be a disciple of the Lord Jesus Christ is to know his discipline.

Dennis Swanberg

Real freedom means to welcome the responsibility it brings, to welcome the God-control it requires, to welcome the discipline that results, to welcome the maturity it creates.

Eugenia Price

Nothing of value is ever acquired without discipline.

Gordan MacDonald

GOD'S WORDS OF WISDOM

I discipline my body and make it my slave.

1 Corinthians 9:27 NASB

God hasn't invited us into a disorderly, unkempt life but into something holy and beautiful—as beautiful on the inside as the outside.

1 Thessalonians 4:7 MSG

Do you not know that those who run in a race all run, but only one receives the prize? Run in such a way that you may win. Everyone who competes in the games exercises self-control in all things.

1 Corinthians 9:24-25 NASB

No discipline seems pleasant at the time, but painful. Later on, however, it produces a harvest of righteousness and peace for those who have been trained by it.

Hebrews 12:11 NIV

SUMMING IT UP

When you take a disciplined approach to your life and your responsibilities, God will reward your good judgment.

GUARD YOUR STEPS BY SETTING A GOOD EXAMPLE

Be an example to the believers in word, in conduct,
in love, in spirit, in faith, in purity.

1 Timothy 4:12 NKJV

How do people know that you're a Christian? Well, you can tell them, of course. And make no mistake about it: talking about your faith in God is a very good thing to do. But simply telling people about Jesus isn't enough. You must also be willing to show people how an extremely devoted Christian (like you) should behave.

Is your life a picture book of your creed? Do your actions line up with your beliefs? Are you willing to practice the philosophy that you preach? If so, congratulations. If not, it's time for a change.

Like it or not, your behavior is a powerful example to others. The question is not whether you will be an example to your family and friends; the question is what kind of example will you be.

Corrie ten Boom advised, "Don't worry about what you do not understand. Worry about what you do understand in the Bible but do not live by." And that's sound advice because your family and friends are always watching . . . and so, for that matter, is God.

> *In every way be an example*
> *of doing good deeds. When you teach,*
> *do it with honesty and seriousness.*
>
> Titus 2:7 NCV

A TIP FOR GUARDING YOUR HEART

Your friends are watching: so be the kind of example that God wants you to be—be a good example.

WORDS OF WISDOM

Integrity of heart is indispensable.

John Calvin

If I take care of my character, my reputation will take care of itself.

D. L. Moody

There is no way to grow a saint overnight. Character, like the oak tree, does not spring up like a mushroom.

Vance Havner

Your light is the truth of the Gospel message itself as well as your witness as to Who Jesus is and what He has done for you. Don't hide it.

Anne Graham Lotz

You can never separate a leader's actions from his character.

John Maxwell

GOD'S WORDS OF WISDOM

In everything you do, stay away from complaining and arguing, so that no one can speak a word of blame against you. You are to live clean, innocent lives as children of God in a dark world full of crooked and perverse people. Let your lives shine brightly before them.

Philippians 2:14-15 NLT

You are the light that gives light to the world. In the same way, you should be a light for other people. Live so that they will see the good things you do and will praise your Father in heaven.

Matthew 5:14,16 NCV

We have around us many people whose lives tell us what faith means. So let us run the race that is before us and never give up. We should remove from our lives anything that would get in the way and the sin that so easily holds us back.

Hebrews 12:1 NCV

SUMMING IT UP

God wants you to be a good example to your family, to your friends, and to the world.

GUARD YOUR STEPS AGAINST IMPULSIVE BEHAVIOR

A person who moves too quickly may go the wrong way.

Proverbs 19:2 NLT

A re you, at times, just a little bit impulsive? Do you occasionally leap before you look? Do you react first and think about your reaction second? If so, God's Word has some advice for you.

In the Bible it's clear that we want to guard our steps and our hearts, we must lead lives of discipline, diligence, and moderation. But the world often tempts us to behave otherwise. Everywhere we turn, it seems, we face powerful temptations to indulge in undisciplined, unruly behaviors—impulsive behaviors that distance us from God.

The Bible instructs us to be disciplined in our thoughts and our actions; it warns us against the dangers

of impulsiveness. Our impulses may lead us astray, but
our heavenly Father will not. So if we're wise, we'll learn
to slow ourselves down, we'll look (and think) before we
leap, and we'll consult God before we make big decisions,
not after.

*An impulsive vow is a trap;
later you'll wish you could get out of it.*

Proverbs 20:25 MSG

A TIP FOR GUARDING YOUR HEART

No so fast! If you're about to do something, but you're
not sure if it's the right thing to do, slow down! It's
better to make a good decision than a fast decision.

WORDS OF WISDOM

Wisdom always waits for the right time to act, while emotion always pushes for action right now.

Joyce Meyer

We will always experience regret when we live for the moment and do not weigh our words and deeds before we give them life.

Lisa Bevere

Zeal without knowledge is always less useful and effective than regulated zeal, and very often is highly dangerous.

St. Bernard of Clairvaux

Periods of anticipation create longing and desire, and the greater the desire, the stronger the passion and more ultimate the fulfillment.

Lisa Bevere

Waiting on God is the same as walking with God toward exciting new rooms of potential and service.

Susan Lenzkes

GOD'S WORDS OF WISDOM

It is a snare for a man to devote rashly something as holy, And afterward to reconsider his vows.

Proverbs 20:25 NKJV

He who is slow to wrath has great understanding, but he who is impulsive exalts folly.

Proverbs 14:29 NKJV

The plans of hard-working people earn a profit, but those who act too quickly become poor.

Proverbs 21:5 NCV

Don't let your spirit rush to be angry, for anger abides in the heart of fools.

Ecclesiastes 7:9 Holman CSB

SUMMING IT UP

If you're a little too impulsive, it's time to slow down, to put your mind in gear, and to start looking more carefully before you leap.

GUARD YOUR STEPS BY CHOOSING WISE ROLE MODELS

The wise are glad to be instructed.

Proverbs 10:8 NLT

Would you like to become a little wiser? Or maybe a lot wiser? If so, then you should make it a point to surround yourself with people who, by their words and their presence, make you a smarter person. But it doesn't stop there. You should also work overtime to avoid hanging out with anybody who encourages you to think foolish thoughts or do foolish things.

Whenever you ask people for advice, it's smart to ask folks who have been there and done that. So, if you want to get real smart real fast, you'll find thoughtful, mature adults who can help you chart your course through life.

Today, as a gift to yourself, select—from your friends, teachers, or family members—at least two mentors whose judgment you trust. Then listen carefully to your mentors' advice and be willing to accept that advice, even if accepting it requires effort, or pain, or both. Consider your mentors to be God's gifts to you. Thank God for those gifts, and use them.

Listen to advice and accept correction,
and in the end you will be wise.

Proverbs 19:20 NCV

A TIP FOR GUARDING YOUR HEART

Rely on the advice of trusted friends and mentors. Proverbs 1:5 makes it clear: "A wise man will hear and increase learning, and a man of understanding will attain wise counsel." (NKJV)

WORDS OF WISDOM

God guides through the counsel of good people.

E. Stanley Jones

It takes a wise person to give good advice, but an even wiser person to take it.

Marie T. Freeman

A single word, if spoken in a friendly spirit, may be sufficient to turn one from dangerous error.

Fanny Crosby

No matter how crazy or nutty your life has seemed, God can make something strong and good out of it. He can help you grow wide branches for others to use as shelter.

Barbara Johnson

God often keeps us on the path by guiding us through the counsel of friends and trusted spiritual advisors.

Bill Hybels

GOD'S WORDS OF WISDOM

*If you help, just help, don't take over; if you teach, stick to
your teaching; if you give encouraging guidance, be careful
that you don't get bossy; if you're put in charge, don't
manipulate; if you're called to give aid to people in distress,
keep your eyes open and be quick to respond; if you work with
the disadvantaged, don't let yourself get irritated with them or
depressed by them. Keep a smile on your face. Love from the
center of who you are; don't fake it. Run for dear life from evil;
hold on for dear life to good.*

Romans 12:7-9 MSG

*The one who walks with the wise will become wise, but a
companion of fools will suffer harm.*

Proverbs 13:20 Holman CSB

*A wise man will hear and increase in learning, and a man of
understanding will acquire wise counsel.*

Proverbs 1:5 NASB

SUMMING IT UP

You need mentors you can trust and emulate. And if
you're not sure what the word emulate means, ask your
mentor.

GUARD YOUR STEPS BY WORKING DILIGENTLY

Concentrate on doing your best for God,
work you won't be ashamed of,
laying out the truth plain and simple.

2 Timothy 2:15 MSG

Have you acquired the habit of doing first things first, or are you one of those people who puts off important work until the last minute? The answer to this simple question will help determine how well you do your work and how much fun you have doing it.

God's Word teaches us the value of hard work. In his second letter to the Thessalonians, Paul warns, " . . . if any would not work, neither should he eat" (3:10 KJV). And the Book of Proverbs proclaims, "One who is slack in his work is brother to one who destroys" (18:9 NIV). In short, God has created a world in which diligence is rewarded and laziness is not. So, whatever it is that you choose to do, do it with commitment, excitement, and vigor. And remember this: Hard work is not simply a proven way to get ahead; it's also part of God's plan for you.

You have countless opportunities to accomplish great things for God—but you should not expect the work to be easy. So pray as if everything depended upon God, but work as if everything depended upon you. When you do, you should expect very big payoffs because when you and God become partners in your work, amazing things happen.

He did it with all his heart. So he prospered.

2 Chronicles 31:21 NKJV

A TIP FOR GUARDING YOUR HEART

Goofing off is contagious. That's why it's important for you to hang out with people who are interested in getting the job done right—and getting it done right now!

WORDS OF WISDOM

We must trust as if it all depended on God and work as if it all depended on us.

C. H. Spurgeon

Thank God every morning when you get up that you have something which must be done, whether you like it or not. Work breeds a hundred virtues that idleness never knows.

Charles Kingsley

It may be that the day of judgment will dawn tomorrow; in that case, we shall gladly stop working for a better tomorrow. But not before.

Dietrich Bonhoeffer

Ordinary work, which is what most of us do most of the time, is ordained by God every bit as much as is the extraordinary.

Elisabeth Elliot

The world does not consider labor a blessing, therefore it flees and hates it, but the pious who fear the Lord labor with a ready and cheerful heart, for they know God's command, and they acknowledge His calling.

Martin Luther

GOD'S WORDS OF WISDOM

But thanks be to God, who gives us the victory through our Lord Jesus Christ. Therefore, my beloved brethren, be steadfast, immovable, always abounding in the work of the Lord, knowing that your labor is not in vain in the Lord.

1 Corinthians 15:57-58 NKJV

Each of us will be rewarded for his own hard work.

1 Corinthians 3:8 TLB

In all the work you are doing, work the best you can. Work as if you were doing it for the Lord, not for people.

Colossians 3:23 NCV

Be strong and brave, and do the work. Don't be afraid or discouraged, because the Lord God, my God, is with you. He will not fail you or leave you."

1 Chronicles 28:20 NCV

SUMMING IT UP

When you find things to do that please God—and when you apply yourself conscientiously to the work at hand—you'll be rewarded.

GUARD YOUR STEPS BY LIVING PURPOSEFULLY

You will show me the path of life;
in Your presence is fullness of joy;
at Your right hand are pleasures forevermore.

Psalm 16:11 NKJV

"What on earth does God intend for me to do with my life?" It's an easy question to ask but, for many of us, a difficult question to answer. Why? Because God's purposes aren't always clear to us. Sometimes we wander aimlessly in a wilderness of our own making. And sometimes, we struggle mightily against God in an unsuccessful attempt to find success and happiness through our own means, not His.

Are you genuinely trying to figure out God's purpose for your life? If so, you can be sure that with God's help, you will eventually discover it. So keep praying, and keep watching. And rest assured: God's got big plans for you . . . very big plans.

To everything there is a season,
a time for every purpose under heaven

Ecclesiastes 3:1 NKJV

A TIP FOR GUARDING YOUR HEART

Discovering God's purpose for your life is continuing education: God's plan is unfolding day by day. If you keep your eyes and your heart open, He'll reveal His plans. God has big things in store for you, but He may have quite a few lessons to teach you before you are fully prepared to do His will and fulfill His purposes.

WORDS OF WISDOM

God wants to revolutionize our lives—by showing us how knowing Him can be the most powerful force to help us become all we want to be.

Bill Hybels

Their distress is due entirely to their deliberate determination to use themselves for a purpose other than God's.

Oswald Chambers

God is more concerned with the direction of your life than with its speed.

Marie T. Freeman

God specializes in things fresh and firsthand. His plans for you this year may outshine those of the past. He's prepared to fill your days with reasons to give Him praise.

Joni Eareckson Tada

Oh Lord, let me not live to be useless.

John Wesley

GOD'S WORDS OF WISDOM

We look at this Son and see the God who cannot be seen. We look at this Son and see God's original purpose in everything created.

Colossians 1:15 MSG

There is one thing I always do. Forgetting the past and straining toward what is ahead, I keep trying to reach the goal and get the prize for which God called me . . . .

Philippians 3:13–14 NCV

Whatever you do, do all to the glory of God.

1 Corinthians 10:31 NKJV

You're sons of Light, daughters of Day. We live under wide open skies and know where we stand. So let's not sleepwalk through life . . .

1 Thessalonians 5:5-6 MSG

SUMMING IT UP

When you gain a clear vision of your purpose for life here on earth—and for life everlasting—your steps will be sure.

GUARD YOUR STEPS AGAINST PEER PRESSURE

Dear friend, don't let this bad example influence you.
Follow only what is good. Remember that those who do
good prove that they are God's children,
and those who do evil prove that they do not know God.

3 John 1:11 NLT

O
ur world is filled with pressures: some good, some bad. The pressures that we feel to follow God's will and to obey His commandments are positive pressures. God places them on our hearts, and He intends that we act in accordance with these feelings. But we also face different pressures, ones that are definitely not from God. When we feel pressured to do things—or even to think thoughts—that lead us away from God, we must beware.

Rick Warren observed, "Those who follow the crowd usually get lost in it." We know these words to be true, but oftentimes we fail to live by them. Instead of trusting God for guidance, we imitate our friends and suffer the consequences. Instead of seeking to please our Father in heaven, we strive to please our peers, with decidedly mixed results. Instead of doing the right thing, we do the "easy" thing or the "popular" thing. And when we do, we pay a high price for our shortsightedness.

Are you satisfied to follow the crowd, or will you follow the One from Galilee? If you sincerely want to please God, you must resist the pressures that society seeks to impose upon you, and you must conform yourself, instead, to God's will, to His path, and to His Son.

> *My son, if sinners entice you,*
> *don't be persuaded.*
>
> Proverbs 1:10 Holman CSB

A Tip for Guarding Your Heart

If you're trying to impress your friends by doing things that your conscience tells you not to do, start paying more attention to your conscience and less attention to your friends.

WORDS OF WISDOM

You will get untold flak for prioritizing God's revealed and present will for your life over man's . . . but, boy, is it worth it.

Beth Moore

Comparison is the root of all feelings of inferiority.

James Dobson

We, as God's people, are not only to stay far away from sin and sinners who would entice us, but we are to be so like our God that we mourn over sin.

Kay Arthur

You should forget about trying to be popular with everybody and start trying to be popular with God Almighty.

Sam Jones

It is comfortable to know that we are responsible to God and not to man. It is a small matter to be judged of man's judgement.

Lottie Moon

GOD'S WORDS OF WISDOM

We must obey God rather than men.

Acts 5:29 Holman CSB

Do not be misled: "Bad company corrupts good character."

1 Corinthians 15:33 NIV

Don't become partners with those who reject God. How can you make a partnership out of right and wrong? That's not partnership; that's war. Is light best friends with dark?

2 Corinthians 6:14 MSG

For am I now trying to win the favor of people, or God? Or am I striving to please people? If I were still trying to please people, I would not be a slave of Christ.

Galatians 1:10 Holman CSB

SUMMING IT UP

A great way to guard your steps is by associating with friends who guard theirs.

GUARD YOUR STEPS WITH WISE PRIORITIES

It's obvious, isn't it? The place where your treasure is,
is the place you will most want to be, and end up being.

Luke 12:34 MSG

"First things first." These words are easy to say, but much harder to put into practice. For busy people living in a demanding world, placing first things first can be difficult indeed. Why? Because so many people are expecting so many things from us!

If you're having trouble prioritizing your day, perhaps you've been trying to organize your life according to your own plans, not God's. A better strategy, of course, is to take your daily obligations and place them in the hands of the One who created you. To do so, you must prioritize your day according to God's commandments, and you must seek His will and His wisdom in all matters. Then, you can face the day with the assurance that the same God who created our universe out of nothingness will help you place first things first in your own life.

Do you feel overwhelmed or confused? Then guard your steps by following in the footsteps of the One from Galilee. Turn the concerns of this day over to God— prayerfully, earnestly, and often. Then, listen for His answer . . . and trust the answer He gives.

First pay attention to me, and then relax.
Now you can take it easy—
you're in good hands.

Proverbs 1:33 MSG

A TIP FOR GUARDING YOUR HEART

Setting priorities may mean saying no. You don't have time to do everything, so it's perfectly okay to say no to the things that mean less so that you'll have time for the things that mean more.

WORDS OF WISDOM

Getting things accomplished isn't nearly as important as taking time for love.

Janette Oke

Have you prayed about your resources lately? Find out how God wants you to use your time and your money. No matter what it costs, forsake all that is not of God.

Kay Arthur

Forgetting your mission leads, inevitably, to getting tangled up in details—details that can take you completely off your path.

Laurie Beth Jones

Your priorities, passions, goals, and fears are shown clearly in the flow of your money.

Dave Ramsey

I have decided not to let my time be used up by people to whom I make no difference while I neglect those for whom I am irreplaceable.

Tony Campolo

GOD'S WORDS OF WISDOM

The thing you should want most is God's kingdom and doing what God wants. Then all these other things you need will be given to you.

Matthew 6:33 NCV

He said to them all, "If anyone desires to come after Me, let him deny himself, and take up his cross daily, and follow Me. For whoever desires to save his life will lose it, but whoever loses his life for My sake will save it."

Luke 9:23-24 NKJV

And I pray this: that your love will keep on growing in knowledge and every kind of discernment, so that you can determine what really matters and can be pure and blameless in the day of Christ.

Philippians 1:9 Holman CSB

SUMMING IT UP

The priorities you choose will dictate the life you live. So choose carefully.

GUARD YOUR STEPS BY WORSHIPPING GOD

Happy are those who hear the joyful call to worship,
for they will walk in the light of your presence, Lord.

Psalm 89:15 NLT

I f you really want to guard your steps, here's something you can do: try worshipping God seven days a week, not just on Sundays.

God has a wonderful plan for your life, and an important part of that plan includes the time that you set aside for praise and worship. Every life, including yours, is based upon some form of worship. The question is not whether you will worship, but what you worship.

If you choose to worship God, you will receive a bountiful harvest of joy, peace, and abundance. But if you distance yourself from God by foolishly worshipping earthly possessions and personal gratification, you're making a huge mistake. So do yourself a favor: Worship God today and every day. Worship Him with sincerity and thanksgiving. Write His name on your heart and rest assured that He, too, has written your name on His.

But seek first his kingdom
and his righteousness,
and all these things will be given to you as well.

Matthew 6:33 NIV

A TIP FOR GUARDING YOUR HEART

Worship reminds you of the awesome power of God. So worship Him daily, and allow Him to work through you every day of the week (not just on Sunday).

WORDS OF WISDOM

Inside the human heart is an undeniable, spiritual instinct to commune with its Creator.

Jim Cymbala

Worship is a daunting task. Each worships differently. But each should worship.

Max Lucado

God asks that we worship Him with our concentrated minds as well as with our wills and emotions. A divided and scattered mind is not effective.

Catherine Marshall

Worship is your spirit responding to God's Spirit.

Rick Warren

It is impossible to worship God and remain unchanged.

Henry Blackaby

GOD'S WORDS OF WISDOM

For it is written, "You shall worship the Lord your God, and Him only you shall serve."

Matthew 4:10 NKJV

God lifted him high and honored him far beyond anyone or anything, ever, so that all created beings in heaven and earth, even those long ago dead and buried, will bow in worship before this Jesus Christ, and call out in praise that he is the Master of all, to the glorious honor of God the Father.

Philippians 2:9-11 MSG

A time is coming and has now come when the true worshipers will worship the Father in spirit and truth, for they are the kind of worshipers the Father seeks. God is spirit, and his worshipers must worship in spirit and in truth.

John 4:23-24 NIV

SUMMING IT UP

When you worship God with a sincere heart, He will guide your steps.

GUARD YOUR STEPS BY WALKING IN CHRIST'S FOOTSTEPS

"Follow Me," Jesus told them,
"and I will make you into fishers of men!"
Immediately they left their nets and followed Him.

Mark 1:17-18 Holman CSB

With whom will you choose to walk today? Will you walk with shortsighted people who honor the ways of the world, or will you walk with the Son of God? Jesus walks with you. Are you walking with Him? Hopefully, you will choose to walk with Him today and every day of your life.

Jesus has called upon believers of every generation (and that includes you) to follow in His footsteps. And God's Word promises that when you follow in Christ's footsteps, you will learn how to live freely and lightly (Matthew 11:28-30).

Jesus doesn't want you to be a run-of-the-mill, follow-the-crowd kind of person. Jesus wants you to be a "new creation" through Him. And that's exactly what you should want for yourself, too. Nothing is more important than your wholehearted commitment to your Creator and to His only begotten Son. Your faith must never be an afterthought; it must be your ultimate priority, your ultimate possession, and you ultimate passion.

You are the recipient of Christ's love. Accept it enthusiastically and share it passionately. Jesus deserves your extreme enthusiasm; the world deserves it; and you deserve the experience of sharing it.

Then Jesus said to His disciples, "If anyone wants to come with Me, he must deny himself, take up his cross, and follow Me."

Matthew 16:24 Holman CSB

A Tip for Guarding Your Heart

Talk is cheap. Real ministry has legs. When it comes to being a disciple, make sure that you back up your words with deeds.

WORDS OF WISDOM

How often it occurs to me, as it must to you, that it is far easier simply to cooperate with God!

Beth Moore

A disciple is a follower of Christ. That means you take on His priorities as your own. His agenda becomes your agenda. His mission becomes your mission.

Charles Stanley

Be filled with the Holy Spirit; join a church where the members believe the Bible and know the Lord; seek the fellowship of other Christians; learn and be nourished by God's Word and His many promises. Conversion is not the end of your journey—it is only the beginning.

Corrie ten Boom

A follower is never greater than his leader; a follower never draws attention to himself.

Franklin Graham

GOD'S WORDS OF WISDOM

Be imitators of God, therefore, as dearly loved children.

Ephesians 5:1 NIV

Work hard, but not just to please your masters when they are watching. As slaves of Christ, do the will of God with all your heart. Work with enthusiasm, as though you were working for the Lord rather than for people.

Ephesians 6:6-7 NLT

If your life honors the name of Jesus, he will honor you.

2 Thessalonians 1:12 MSG

All of us who look forward to his Coming stay ready, with the glistening purity of Jesus' life as a model for our own.

1 John 3:3 MSG

SUMMING IT UP

Jesus has invited you to become His disciple. If you accept His invitation—and if you obey His commandments—you will be protected and blessed.

PART 4

GUARD YOUR HEART

*Above all else, guard your heart, for it affects
everything you do. Avoid all perverse talk;
stay far from corrupt speech. Look straight ahead,
and fix your eyes on what lies before you.
Mark out a straight path for your feet; then stick
to the path and stay safe. Don't get sidetracked;
keep your feet from following evil.*

Proverbs 4:23 NLT

Jesus' Principles of Prayer

And when you pray, do not be like the hypocrites, for they love to pray standing in the synagogues and on the street corners to be seen by men. I tell you the truth, they have received their reward in full. But when you pray, go into your room, close the door and pray to your Father, who is unseen. Then your Father, who sees what is done in secret, will reward you. And when you pray, do not keep on babbling like pagans, for they think they will be heard because of their many words. Do not be like them, for your Father knows what you need before you ask him.

Matthew 6:5-8 NIV

If you sincerely wish to guard your heart, no discipline is more important than the discipline of prayer. In the sixth chapter of Matthew, Jesus offers the Bible's first extensive instructions regarding prayer. It is here that Jesus offers five principles about prayer that still apply.

Principle #1: Pray Regularly. Jesus began His lesson on prayer with the words, "And when you pray . . . " He did not say "if you pray." Prayer was assumed to be a regular daily activity for Christians. In truth, the Christian life cannot be maintained without consistent daily prayer.

Many Christians talk about their "prayer life." Yet God is not as interested in our having "prayer lives" as He is in our having "lives of prayer." And make no mistake: there's a big difference. A "prayer life" indicates that we divide our daily activities into times of prayer and times of non-prayer. What God prefers is that the entirety of a Christian's life should become a constant prayer lifted to Him—every activity dedicated to Him, every part of the day an act of worship.

Principle #2: Pray Privately. Jesus teaches that our times of protracted, concentrated prayer are not to be public spectacles, but are to be private. He admonishes us to go into our rooms, to close the door, and to talk to our Father who is unseen.

Does this mean that we are to never pray publicly? No, but it does mean that most of our prayers are to be private communications, just between God and us.

Some folks may say, "Well, I pray with my family." And, of course, that's an admirable activity. Others may say, "I am in a prayer group at church." And once again, God will be pleased. But nothing should obscure the fact that the majority of our concentrated prayer times are to be private.

Principle #3: Have a Time and Place for Prayer. What we schedule, we do. What we don't schedule, we may never get around to doing. So it's best to set aside a specific time for concentrated prayer.

Jesus had a set time of concentrated prayer—the early morning. Not a morning person? Then try the evening, or maybe during your lunch break. But whatever you do, have a regular, daily time of prayer . . . and have a place.

Jesus prayed outdoors; maybe you find that too distracting. If so, find a room where you can shut the door and pray. Do whatever works for you, but make certain that you have a specific place and time each day when you do nothing, absolutely nothing, but talk to the Father.

Principle #4: Prayer Is Rewarded. We sometimes baulk at the idea that we will be rewarded for doing what we consider to be our duty. Yet if Jesus did not want us to know about the rewards of prayer, He would not have told us that "your Father, who sees what is done in secret, will reward you" (Matthew 6:6).

Do these rewards come now or later? Of course, there may be many earthly rewards for prayer; and we most assuredly benefit from the blessings that arise from the act of praying. But we can also be certain that our prayers will be rewarded in heaven.

Principle #5: Keep It Simple. Jesus said that we are not to pray, "babbling like pagans, for they think they will be heard because of their many words." He tells us that our Father knows what we need before we ask Him. So, we can keep our prayers short, sweet, and simple. We needn't try to impress God by fancy speeches or lengthy lectures. God isn't concerned with the eloquence of our words, which, by the way, is a very good thing. That means that all of us can talk intimately with God . . . and He always understands.

A TIP FOR GUARDING YOUR HEART

Eyelids Closed . . . Or Not! When you are praying, the position of your eyelids makes little or no difference. Of course, it's good to close your eyes and bow your head whenever you can, but it's also good to offer quick prayers to God with your eyes—and your heart—wide open.

WORDS OF WISDOM

It is well said that neglected prayer is the birth-place of all evil.

C. H. Spurgeon

Obedience is the master key to effective prayer.

Billy Graham

Prayer guards hearts and minds and causes God to bring peace out of chaos.

Beth Moore

Allow your dreams a place in your prayers and plans. God-given dreams can help you move into the future He is preparing for you.

Barbara Johnson

Those who know God the best are the richest and most powerful in prayer. Little acquaintance with God, and strangeness and coldness to Him, make prayer a rare and feeble thing.

E. M. Bounds

GOD'S WORDS OF WISDOM

*Rejoice always, pray without ceasing, in everything give
thanks; for this is the will of God in Christ Jesus for you.*

1 Thessalonians 5:16-18 NKJV

*I want men everywhere to lift up holy hands in prayer, without
anger or disputing.*

1 Timothy 2:8 NIV

*If my people who are called by my name, will humble
themselves and pray and seek my face and turn from their
wicked ways, then will I hear from heaven and will forgive their
sin and will heal their land.*

2 Chronicles 7:14 NIV

*"Relax, Daniel,' he continued, 'don't be afraid. From
the moment you decided to humble yourself to receive
understanding, your prayer was heard, and I set out to come to
you.'"*

Daniel 10:12 MSG

SUMMING IT UP

Prayer changes things—and you—so pray.

ABOVE ALL ELSE GUARD YOUR HEART

Above all else, guard your heart,
for it affects everything you do.

Proverbs 4:23 NLT

There's simply no way around it: if you want to guard your heart, you simply must obey God's commandments. There are no shortcuts and no loopholes—to be a faithful Christian, you must be an obedient Christian.

Would you like to experience God's peace and His blessings? Then obey Him. When you're faced with a difficult choice or a powerful temptation, seek God's counsel and trust the counsel He gives. Invite God into your heart and live according to His commandments. When you do, you will be blessed today, tomorrow, and forever.

God has given you a guidebook for righteous living called the Holy Bible. It contains thorough instructions which, if followed, lead to fulfillment and salvation. But, if you choose to ignore God's commandments, the results are as predictable as they are tragic.

So here's a surefire formula for a happy, abundant life: live righteously.

And for further instructions, read the manual.

*Walk in a manner worthy of the God
who calls you into His own kingdom and glory.*

1 Thessalonians 2:12 NASB

A TIP FOR GUARDING YOUR HEART

Today, consider the value of living a life that is pleasing to God. And while you're at it, think about the rewards that are likely to be yours when you do the right thing day in and day out.

WORDS OF WISDOM

A man who lives right, and is right, has more power in his silence than another has by his words.

Phillips Brooks

Holiness is not God's asking us to be "good"; it is an invitation to be "His."

Lisa Bevere

As you walk by faith, you live a righteous life, for righteousness is always by faith.

Kay Arthur

If we don't hunger and thirst after righteousness, we'll become anemic and feel miserable in our Christian experience.

Franklin Graham

A life lived in God is not lived on the plane of feelings, but of the will.

Elisabeth Elliot

GOD'S WORDS OF WISDOM

Run away from infantile indulgence. Run after mature righteousness—faith, love, peace—joining those who are in honest and serious prayer before God.

2 Timothy 2:22 MSG

And you shall do what is right and good in the sight of the Lord, that it may be well with you.

Deuteronomy 6:18 NKJV

For the eyes of the Lord are on the righteous, and His ears are open to their prayers; but the face of the Lord is against those who do evil.

1 Peter 3:12 NKJV

Discipline yourself for the purpose of godliness.

1 Timothy 4:7 NASB

SUMMING IT UP

Because God is just, He rewards good behavior just as surely as He punishes sin. And there aren't any loopholes.

GUARD YOUR HEART BY GUARDING YOUR THOUGHTS

Those who are pure in their thinking are happy,
because they will be with God.

Matthew 5:8 NCV

Here's something to think about: if you want to guard your heart, you must also guard your thoughts. Why? Because thoughts are intensely powerful things. Your thoughts have the power to lift you up or drag you down; they have the power to energize you or deplete you, to inspire you to greater accomplishments, or to make those accomplishments impossible.

The Bible teaches you to guard your thoughts against things that are hurtful or wrong, yet sometimes you'll be tempted to let your thoughts run wild, especially if those thoughts are of the negative variety.

If you've acquired the habit of thinking constructively about yourself and your circumstances, congratulations.

But if you're mired in the mental quicksand of negativity—or if your mind has been hijacked by all those false messages that the world keeps pumping out—it's now time to change your thoughts, and by doing so, your life.

It is the thoughts and intents of the heart
that shape a person's life.

John Eldredge

A TIP FOR GUARDING YOUR HEART

Good thoughts create good deeds. Good thoughts lead to good deeds and bad thoughts lead elsewhere. So guard your thoughts accordingly.

WORDS OF WISDOM

As we have by faith said no to sin, so we should by faith say yes to God and set our minds on things above, where Christ is seated in the heavenlies.

Vonette Bright

No more imperfect thoughts. No more sad memories. No more ignorance. My redeemed body will have a redeemed mind. Grant me a foretaste of that perfect mind as you mirror your thoughts in me today.

Joni Eareckson Tada

The things we think are the things that feed our souls. If we think on pure and lovely things, we shall grow pure and lovely like them; and the converse is equally true.

Hannah Whitall Smith

Your thoughts are the determining factor as to whose mold you are conformed to. Control your thoughts and you control the direction of your life.

Charles Stanley

GOD'S WORDS OF WISDOM

Dear friend, guard Clear Thinking and Common Sense with your life; don't for a minute lose sight of them. They'll keep your soul alive and well, they'll keep you fit and attractive.

Proverbs 3:21-22 MSG

So prepare your minds for service and have self-control.

1 Peter 1:13 NCV

Come near to God, and God will come near to you. You sinners, clean sin out of your lives. You who are trying to follow God and the world at the same time, make your thinking pure.

James 4:8 NCV

Brothers, don't be childish in your thinking, but be infants in evil and adult in your thinking.

1 Corinthians 14:20 Holman CSB

SUMMING IT UP

Your thoughts have the power to lift you up or bring you down, so you should guard your thoughts very carefully.

GUARD YOUR HEART DURING TOUGH TIMES

When you go through deep waters and great trouble,
I will be with you. When you go through the rivers of
difficulty, you will not drown! When you walk through the fire
of oppression, you will not be burned up; the flames will not
consume you. For I am the Lord, your God . . . .

Isaiah 43:2-3 NLT

The Bible promises this: tough times are temporary, but God's love is not—God's love lasts forever. So what does that mean to you? Just this: From time to time, everybody faces tough times, and so will you. And when tough times arrive, God will always stand ready to protect you and heal you.

Psalm 147 promises, "He heals the brokenhearted" (v. 3, NIV), but Psalm 147 doesn't say that He heals them instantly. Usually, it takes time (and maybe even a little help from you) for God to fix things. So if you're facing tough times, face them with God by your side. If you find yourself in any kind of trouble, pray about it and ask God for help. And be patient. God will work things out, just as He has promised, but He will do it in His own way and in His own time.

*The LORD also will be a stronghold
for the oppressed,
a stronghold in times of trouble.*

Psalm 9:9 NASB

A TIP FOR GUARDING YOUR HEART

Talk about it . . . If you're having tough times, don't hit the panic button and don't keep everything bottled up inside. Talk things over with people you can really trust. And if your troubles seem overwhelming, be willing to seek help—starting, of course, with your parents and your pastor.

WORDS OF WISDOM

Life will be made or broken at the place where we meet and deal with obstacles.

E. Stanley Jones

Unbelief puts our circumstances between us and God. Faith puts God between us and our circumstances.

F. B. Meyer

One sees great things from the valley; only small things from the peak.

G. K. Chesterton

Even in the winter, even in the midst of the storm, the sun is still there. Somewhere, up above the clouds, it still shines and warms and pulls at the life buried deep inside the brown branches and frozen earth. The sun is there! Spring will come.

Gloria Gaither

What is the difference between an obstacle and an opportunity? Our attitude toward it. Every opportunity has a difficulty, and every difficulty has an opportunity.

J. Sidlow Baxter

GOD'S WORDS OF WISDOM

You pulled me from the brink of death, my feet from the cliff-edge of doom. Now I stroll at leisure with God in the sunlit fields of life.

Psalm 56:13 MSG

Don't fret or worry. Instead of worrying, pray. Let petitions and praises shape your worries into prayers, letting God know your concerns. Before you know it, a sense of God's wholeness, everything coming together for good, will come and settle you down.

Philippians 4:6-7 MSG

We also have joy with our troubles, because we know that these troubles produce patience. And patience produces character, and character produces hope.

Romans 5:3-4 NCV

SUMMING IT UP

Tough times are temporary; God is forever. So when tough times arrive, trust God.

GUARD YOUR HEART WITH WISDOM

How much better to get wisdom than gold!
And to get understanding is to be chosen rather than silver.

Proverbs 16:16 NKJV

Are you and your friends wise guys and girls? And, are you striving to help each other become a little wiser every day? Hopefully so.

All of us would like to be wise, but not all of us are willing to do the work that is required to become wise. Why? Because wisdom isn't free—it takes time and effort to acquire.

To become wise, we must seek God's wisdom and live according to His Word. To become wise, we must seek wisdom with consistency and purpose. To become wise, we must not only learn the lessons of the Christian life, we must also live by them (and hang out with people who do likewise).

If you sincerely desire to become wise—and if you seek to share your hard-earned wisdom with others—your actions must give credence to your words. The best way to share one's wisdom—perhaps the only way—is not by words, but by example.

Wisdom is like a savings account: If you add to it consistently, then eventually you'll have a great sum. The secret to success is consistency. Do you seek wisdom? Then seek it every day, and seek it in the right place. That place, of course, is, first and foremost, the Word of God.

Happy is the person who finds wisdom,
the one who gets understanding.

Proverbs 3:13 NCV

A TIP FOR GUARDING YOUR HEART

If you're looking for wisdom, the book of Proverbs is a wonderful place to start. It has 31 chapters, one for each day of the month. If you read Proverbs regularly, and if you take its teachings to heart, you'll gain timeless wisdom from God's unchanging Word.

WORDS OF WISDOM

Wisdom is the God-given ability to see life with rare objectivity and to handle life with rare stability.

Charles Swindoll

Wisdom is knowledge applied. Head knowledge is useless on the battlefield. Knowledge stamped on the heart makes one wise.

Beth Moore

When you and I are related to Jesus Christ, our strength and wisdom and peace and joy and love and hope may run out, but His life rushes in to keep us filled to the brim. We are showered with blessings, not because of anything we have or have not done, but simply because of Him.

Anne Graham Lotz

The more wisdom enters our hearts, the more we will be able to trust our hearts in difficult situations.

John Eldredge

Patience is the companion of wisdom.

St. Augustine

GOD'S WORDS OF WISDOM

Anyone who listens to my teaching and obeys me is wise, like a person who builds a house on solid rock. Though the rain comes in torrents and the floodwaters rise and the winds beat against that house, it won't collapse, because it is built on rock.

Matthew 7:24–25 NLT

But the wisdom that is from above is first pure, then peaceable, gentle, willing to yield, full of mercy and good fruits, without partiality and without hypocrisy.

James 3:17 NKJV

The Lord says, "I will make you wise and show you where to go. I will guide you and watch over you."

Psalm 32:8 NCV

SUMMING IT UP

If you own a Bible, you have ready access to God's wisdom. Your job is to read, to understand, and to apply His teachings to your life . . . starting now and ending never.

GUARD YOUR HEART AGAINST ADDICTION

Be sober! Be on the alert!
Your adversary the Devil is prowling around
like a roaring lion, looking for anyone he can devour.

1 Peter 5:8 Holman CSB

Ours is a society that glamorizes the use of drugs, alcohol, cigarettes, and other addictive substances. Why? The answer can be summed up in one word: money. Simply put, addictive substances are big money makers, so suppliers (of both legal and illegal substances) work overtime to make certain that people like you sample their products. The suppliers need a steady stream of new customers because the old ones are dying off (fast), so they engage in a no-holds-barred struggle to find new users—or more accurately, new abusers.

The dictionary defines addiction as "the compulsive need for a habit-forming substance; the condition of being habitually and compulsively occupied with something." That definition is accurate, but incomplete. For

Christians, addiction has an additional meaning: it means compulsively worshipping something other than God.

Unless you're living on a deserted island, you know people who are full-blown addicts—probably lots of people. If you, or someone you love, is suffering from the blight of addiction, remember this: Help is available. Plenty of people have experienced addiction and lived to tell about it . . . so don't give up hope.

And if you're one of those fortunate people who hasn't started experimenting with addictive substances, please continue to guard your heart, your body, your mind, and your life. If you do, you'll spare yourself a lifetime of headaches and heartaches.

You shall have no other gods before Me.

Exodus 20:3 NKJV

A TIP FOR GUARDING YOUR HEART

Make Jesus your highest priority, and ask Him to help you overcome any obsessions that might distance you from Him.

WORDS OF WISDOM

The soul that journeys to God, but doesn't shake off its cares and quiet its appetites, is like someone who drags a cart uphill.

St. John of the Cross

Above all, we must be especially alert against the beginnings of temptation, for the enemy is more easily conquered if he is refused admittance to the mind and is met beyond the threshold when he knocks.

Thomas à Kempis

Addiction is the most powerful psychic enemy of humanity's desire for God.

Gerald May

We are meant to be addicted to God, but we develop secondary addictions that temporarily appear to fix our problem.

Edward M. Berckman

It all starts in the mind and the mouth and springs from a lack of balance and self-discipline.

Joyce Meyer

GOD'S WORDS OF WISDOM

Death is the reward of an undisciplined life; your foolish decisions trap you in a dead end.

Proverbs 5:23 MSG

Yet in all these things we are more than conquerors through Him who loved us.

Romans 8:37 NKJV

For we do not have a High Priest who cannot sympathize with our weaknesses, but was in all points tempted as we are, yet without sin. Let us therefore come boldly to the throne of grace, that we may obtain mercy and find grace to help in time of need.

Hebrews 4:15-16 NKJV

SUMMING IT UP

Addictive substances and compulsive behaviors have the power to destroy your life. It's up to you to make sure that they don't.

GUARD YOUR HEART WITH A POSITIVE ATTITUDE

And now, dear brothers and sisters, let me say one more thing as I close this letter. Fix your thoughts on what is true and honorable and right. Think about things that are pure and lovely and admirable. Think about things that are excellent and worthy of praise.

Philippians 4:8 NLT

One way to guard your heart is by making sure that your attitude is pleasing to God. How will you direct your thoughts today? Will you obey the words of Philippians 4:8 by dwelling upon those things that are honorable and true? Or will you allow your thoughts to be hijacked by the negativity that seems to dominate our troubled world?

Are you fearful, angry, bored, or worried? Are you so preoccupied with the concerns of this day that you fail to thank God for the promise of eternity? Are you confused, bitter, or pessimistic? If so, God wants you to think long and hard about the way you've been thinking.

God intends that you experience joy and abundance, but He will not force His joy upon you; you must claim it for yourself. So, today and every day hereafter, celebrate this life that God has given you by focusing your thoughts and your energies upon "excellent and worthy of praise." Today, count your blessings instead of your hardships. And thank the Giver of all things good for gifts that are simply too numerous to count.

> *Set your mind on things above,*
> *not on things on the earth.*
>
> *Colossians 3:2 NKJV*

A TIP FOR GUARDING YOUR HEART

Focus on Getting Your Attitude Right: If you're a victim of stinkin' thinkin', you'll never win the big ones. So if you want to be a winner, make sure that your attitude enhances your chances of winning.

WORDS OF WISDOM

The difference between winning and losing is how we choose to react to disappointment.

Barbara Johnson

I have witnessed many attitudes make a positive turnaround through prayer.

John Maxwell

It's your choice: you can either count your blessings or recount your disappointments.

Jim Gallery

The reference point for the Christian is the Bible. All values, judgments, and attitudes must be gauged in relationship to this reference point.

Ruth Bell Graham

Attitude is the mind's paintbrush; it can color any situation.

Barbara Johnson

GOD'S WORDS OF WISDOM

So prepare your minds for service and have self-control.

1 Peter 1:13 NCV

Come near to God, and God will come near to you. You sinners, clean sin out of your lives. You who are trying to follow God and the world at the same time, make your thinking pure.

James 4:8 NCV

Those who are pure in their thinking are happy, because they will be with God.

Matthew 5:8 NCV

For God has not given us a spirit of fear, but of power and of love and of a sound mind.

2 Timothy 1:7 NLT

SUMMING IT UP

A positive attitude leads to positive results; a negative attitude leads elsewhere.

GUARD YOUR HEART
WITH BIBLE STUDY

*There's nothing like the written Word of God for showing you
the way to salvation through faith in Christ Jesus. Every part
of Scripture is God-breathed and useful one way or another,
showing us truth, exposing our rebellion, correcting our
mistakes, training us to live God's way. Through the Word we
are put together and shaped up for the tasks God has for us.*

2 Timothy 3:15-17 MSG

A surefire, time-tested way to guard your heart is by
studying God's Word.

Do you read your Bible a lot . . . or not? The
answer to this simple question will determine, to a
surprising extent, the quality of your decisions, the quality
of your life, and the direction of your faith.

You (and only you) must decide whether God's Word
will be a bright spotlight that guides your path every day
or a tiny nightlight that occasionally flickers in the dark.
The decision to study the Bible—or not—is an important

choice; how you choose to use your Bible will have a profound impact on your future.

The Bible is unlike any other book. It is a priceless gift from your Creator, a tool that God intends for you to use in every aspect of your life. And, it contains promises upon which you, as a Christian, can and must depend.

God's Word can be a roadmap to success and spiritual abundance. Make it your roadmap. God's wisdom can be a light to guide your steps. Claim it as your light today, tomorrow, and every day of your life—and then walk confidently in the footsteps of God's only begotten Son.

A TIP FOR GUARDING YOUR HEART

Trust God's Word: Charles Swindoll writes, "There are four words I wish we would never forget, and they are, 'God keeps His word.'" And remember: When it comes to studying God's Word, school is always in session.

WORDS OF WISDOM

God can see clearly no matter how dark or foggy the night is. Trust His Word to guide you safely home.

Lisa Whelchel

Words fail to express my love for this holy Book, my gratitude for its author, for His love and goodness. How shall I thank him for it?

Lottie Moon

The Bible became a living book and a guide for my life.

Vonette Bright

A thorough knowledge of the Bible is worth more than a college education.

Theodore Roosevelt

The Bible is God's Word, given to us by God Himself so we can know Him and His will for our lives.

Billy Graham

GOD'S WORDS OF WISDOM

Your word is a lamp to my feet and a light for my path.

Psalm 119:105 NIV

Blessed are those who hunger and thirst for righteousness, For they shall be filled.

Matthew 5:6 NKJV

Jesus answered, "It is written: 'Man does not live by bread alone, but on every word that comes from the mouth of God.'"

Matthew 4:4 NIV

So then faith comes by hearing, and hearing by the word of God.

Romans 10:17 NKJV

The words of the Lord are pure words, like silver tried in a furnace . . . .

Psalm 12:6 NKJV

SUMMING IT UP

God's Word can guide your steps and guard your heart. Let your Bible be your guide.

GUARD YOUR HEART BY ACCEPTING GOD'S PEACE

The peace of God, which surpasses all understanding, will guard your hearts and minds through Christ Jesus.

Philippians 4:7 NKJV

You can guard your heart by accepting God's peace, but sometimes, it's hard. Peace can be a scarce commodity in this noisy, dog-eat-dog, 21st Century world. How, then, can you experience God's peace? By turning your heart and your life over to Him.

Jesus offers peace, not as the world gives, but as He alone gives. You, as human being with free will, can accept His peace or ignore it. When you allow the peace of Jesus Christ to enter your heart, your life will be transformed. And then, because you possess the gift of peace, you can share that gift with fellow Christians, family members, and friends. If, on the other hand, you choose to ignore God's gift—for whatever reason—you simply cannot share what you do not possess.

Today, as a gift to yourself, to your family, and to your friends, claim the inner peace that is your spiritual birthright: the peace of Jesus Christ. It is offered freely; it has been paid for in full; it is yours for the asking. So ask. And then share.

> *If it is possible, as far as it depends on you,*
> *live at peace with everyone.*
>
> *Romans 12:18 NIV*

A TIP FOR GUARDING YOUR HEART

Peace in the present moment. Does peace seem to be a distant promise? It is not. God's peace is available to you this very moment if you place absolute trust in Him.

The better acquainted you become with God, the less tensions you feel and the more peace you possess.

Charles Allen

I believe that in every time and place, it is within our power to acquiesce in the will of God—and what peace it brings to do so!

Elisabeth Elliot

His life is our light—our purpose and meaning and reason for living.

Anne Graham Lotz

The fruit of our placing all things in God's hands is the presence of His abiding peace in our hearts.

Hannah Whitall Smith

Love comes while we rest against our Father's chest. Joy comes when we catch the rhythms of His heart. Peace comes when we live in harmony with those rhythms.

Ken Gire

GOD'S WORDS OF WISDOM

Blessed are the peacemakers, for they will be called sons of God.

Matthew 5:9 NIV

You, Lord, give true peace to those who depend on you, because they trust you.

Isaiah 26:3 NCV

If your sinful nature controls your mind, there is death. But if the Holy Spirit controls your mind, there is life and peace.

Romans 8:6 NLT

Peace I leave with you, My peace I give to you; not as the world gives do I give to you. Let not your heart be troubled, neither let it be afraid.

John 14:27 NKJV

SUMMING IT UP

God's peace surpasses human understanding. When you accept His peace, it will revolutionize your life.

GUARD YOUR HEART AGAINST THE TEMPTATION TO JUDGE

Do not judge, and you will not be judged.
Do not condemn, and you will not be condemned.
Forgive, and you will be forgiven.

Luke 6:37 Holman CSB

Would you like a formula for being unhappy? Here it is: spend as much time as you can judging other people. But if you'd rather be happy—and if you'd rather guard your heart by obeying your Heavenly Father—please remember this: in matters of judgment, God certainly does not need your help. Why? Because God is perfectly capable of judging the human heart . . . while you are not.

God is perfect; we are not. So none of us is qualified to "cast the first stone." Thankfully, God has forgiven us, and we, too, must forgive others. It's just not that complicated!

Have you developed the bad habit of behaving yourself like an amateur judge and jury, assigning blame and condemnation wherever you go? If so, it's time to grow up and obey God. When it comes to judging everything and everybody, God doesn't need your help . . . and He doesn't want it.

You, therefore, have no excuse,
you who pass judgment on someone else,
for at whatever point you judge the other,
you are condemning yourself.

Romans 2:1 NIV

A TIP FOR GUARDING YOUR HEART

Your ability to judge others requires a divine insight that you simply don't have. So, do everybody (including yourself) a favor: don't judge.

WORDS OF WISDOM

Being critical of others, including God, is one way we try to avoid facing and judging our own sins.

Warren Wiersbe

Don't judge other people more harshly than you want God to judge you.

Marie T. Freeman

Turn your attention upon yourself and beware of judging the deeds of other men, for in judging others a man labors vainly, often makes mistakes, and easily sins; whereas, in judging and taking stock of himself he does something that is always profitable.

Thomas à Kempis

Only Christ can free us from the prison of legalism, and then only if we are willing to be freed.

Madeleine L'Engle

Judging draws the judgment of others.

Catherine Marshall

GOD'S WORDS OF WISDOM

So when they continued asking him, he lifted up himself, and said unto them, He that is without sin among you, let him first cast a stone at her.

John 8:7 KJV

Speak and act as those who will be judged by the law of freedom. For judgment is without mercy to the one who hasn't shown mercy. Mercy triumphs over judgment.

James 2:12-13 Holman CSB

Do not judge, or you too will be judged. For in the same way you judge others, you will be judged, and with the measure you use, it will be measured to you.

Matthew 7:1 NIV

SUMMING IT UP

If you're setting yourself up to be the judge and jury over other people, watch out! God will judge you in the same way you judge them. So don't be too hard on other people (unless, of course, you want God to be exactly that hard on you).

GUARD YOUR HEART AGAINST WORRY

Don't worry about anything, but in everything,
through prayer and petition with thanksgiving,
let your requests be made known to God.

Philippians 4:6 Holman CSB

Are you willing to guard your heart against worry? Well, that's what the Bible says you should do. When you're worried, there are two places you should take your concerns: to the people who love you and to God. When troubles arise (as they will from time to time), it helps to talk things over with parents, grandparents, concerned adults, and trusted friends. But you shouldn't stop there: you should also have a heart-to-heart talk with God.

If you're worried about something, pray about it. Remember that God is always listening, and He always wants to hear from you.

So when you're upset about your life or your future, try this simple plan: talk and pray. Talk openly to the people who love you, and pray to the Heavenly Father who made you. The more you talk and the more you pray, the better you'll feel.

Jesus said,
"Don't let your hearts be troubled.
Trust in God, and trust in me."

John 14:1 NCV

A TIP FOR GUARDING YOUR HEART

Remember: This, too, will pass. And remember that it will pass more quickly if you spend more time solving problems and less time fretting over them.

WORDS OF WISDOM

This life of faith, then, consists in just this—being a child in the Father's house. Let the ways of childish confidence and freedom from care, which so please you and win your heart when you observe your own little ones, teach you what you should be in your attitude toward God.

Hannah Whitall Smith

Pray, and let God worry.

Martin Luther

Today is mine. Tomorrow is none of my business. If I peer anxiously into the fog of the future, I will strain my spiritual eyes so that I will not see clearly what is required of me now.

Elisabeth Elliott

Worry and anxiety are sand in the machinery of life; faith is the oil.

E. Stanley Jones

Today is the tomorrow we worried about yesterday.

Dennis Swanberg

GOD'S WORDS OF WISDOM

Yea, though I walk through the valley of the shadow of death, I will fear no evil: for thou art with me; thy rod and thy staff they comfort me.

Psalm 23:4 KJV

Come to Me, all you who labor and are heavy laden, and I will give you rest. Take My yoke upon you and learn from Me, for I am gentle and lowly in heart, and you will find rest for your souls. For My yoke is easy and My burden is light.

Matthew 11:28-30 NKJV

Peace I leave with you, my peace I give unto you: not as the world giveth, give I unto you. Let not your heart be troubled, neither let it be afraid.

John 14:27 KJV

SUMMING IT UP

You have worries, but God has solutions. Your challenge it to trust Him to solve the problems that you can't.

GUARD YOUR HEART BY PUTTING GOD FIRST

You shall have no other gods before Me.

Exodus 20:3 NKJV

By putting God first, you guard your heart. By putting Him second, third, or fourth, you put yourself at risk.

Who is in charge of your heart? Is it God, or is it something else? Have you given Christ your heart, your soul, your talents, your time, and your testimony? Or are you giving Him little more than a few hours each Sunday morning?

In the book of Exodus, God warns that we should place no gods before Him. Yet all too often, we place our Lord in a lesser position as we worship other things. When we unwittingly place possessions or relationships above our love for the Creator, we create big problems for ourselves.

Does God rule your heart? Make certain that the honest answer to this question is a resounding yes. In the life of every faithful believer, God comes first. And that's precisely the place that He deserves in your heart.

> Huge as this universe is,
> God has complete power over it,
> as you have with a ball
> which you toss in your hand.
>
> *C. H. Spurgeon*

A TIP FOR GUARDING YOUR HEART

Focus on God: If you put your obligations to other people (or your desire for stuff) above your desire to please God, you're making a king-sized mistake. So as you're making plans for the day ahead, put God in the #1 slot. When you do, you'll make better choices, and you'll earn bigger rewards.

WORDS OF WISDOM

Our concepts of measurement embrace mountains and men, atoms and stars, gravity, energy, numbers, speed, but never God. We cannot speak of measure or amount or size or weight and at the same time be speaking of God, for these tell of degrees and there are no degrees in God. All that he is he is without growth or addition or development.

A. W. Tozer

I can see how it might be possible for a man to look down upon the earth and be an atheist, but I cannot conceive how he could look up into the heavens and say there is no God.

Abraham Lincoln

I lived with Indians who made pots out of clay which they used for cooking. Nobody was interested in the pot. Everybody was interested in what was inside. The same clay taken out of the same riverbed, always made in the same design, nothing special about it. Well, I'm a clay pot, and let me not forget it. But, the excellency of the power is of God and not us.

Elisabeth Elliot

GOD'S WORDS OF WISDOM

The fool says in his heart, "God does not exist."

Psalm 14:1 Holman CSB

God is love, and the one who remains in love remains in God, and God remains in him.

1 John 4:16 Holman CSB

Be still, and know that I am God . . . .

Psalm 46:10 KJV

For the Lord your God is the God of gods and Lord of lords, the great, mighty, and awesome God.

Deuteronomy 10:17 Holman CSB

God is Spirit, and those who worship Him must worship in spirit and truth.

John 4:24 Holman CSB

SUMMING IT UP

God deserves first place in your life . . . and you deserve the experience of putting Him there.

ABOVE ALL ELSE:
YOUR RELATIONSHIP
WITH CHRIST

For God so loved the world that he gave his only Son,
so that everyone who believes in him
will not perish but have eternal life.

John 3:16 NLT

Ours is not a distant God. Ours is a God who understands—far better than we ever could—the essence of what it means to be human. How marvelous it is that God became a man and walked among us. Had He not chosen to do so, we might feel removed from a distant Creator.

God understands our hopes, our fears, and our temptations. He understands what it means to be angry and what it costs to forgive. He knows the heart, the conscience, and the soul of every person who has ever lived, including you. And God has a plan of salvation that is intended for you. Accept it. Accept God's gift through the person of His Son Christ Jesus, and then rest assured: God walked among us so that you might have eternal life; amazing though it may seem, He did it for you.

These things I have written to you
who believe in the name of the Son of God,
that you may know that you have eternal life.

1 John 5:13 NKJV

A TIP FOR GUARDING YOUR HEART

People love talking about religion, and everybody has their own opinions, but ultimately only one opinion counts . . . God's. Talk to your friends about God's promise of eternal life—what that promise means to you and what it should mean to them.

WORDS OF WISDOM

Teach us to set our hopes on heaven, to hold firmly to the promise of eternal life, so that we can withstand the struggles and storms of this world.

Max Lucado

Those of us who know the wonderful grace of redemption look forward to an eternity with God, when all things will be made new, when all our longings will at last find ultimate and final satisfaction.

Joseph Stowell

As I contemplate all the sacrifices required in order to live a life that is totally focused on Jesus Christ and His eternal kingdom, the joy seeps out of my heart onto my face in a smile of deep satisfaction.

Anne Graham Lotz

The damage done to us on this earth will never find its way into that safe city. We can relax, we can rest, and though some of us can hardly imagine it, we can prepare to feel safe and secure for all of eternity.

Bill Hybels

GOD'S WORDS OF WISDOM

*And this is the testimony: that God has given us eternal life,
and this life is in His Son. He who has the Son has life; he who
does not have the Son of God does not have life.*

1 John 5:11-12 NKJV

*We do not want you to be uninformed, brothers, concerning
those who are asleep, so that you will not grieve like the rest,
who have no hope. Since we believe that Jesus died and rose
again, in the same way God will bring with Him those who
have fallen asleep through Jesus.*

1 Thessalonians 4:13-14 Holman CSB

*Pursue righteousness, godliness, faith, love, endurance, and
gentleness. Fight the good fight for the faith; take hold of eternal
life, to which you were called and have made a good confession
before many witnesses.*

1 Timothy 6:11-12 Holman CSB

SUMMING IT UP

God offers you a priceless gift: the gift of eternal life. If
you have not already done so, accept God's gift today—
tomorrow may be too late.

Tim Way has been on staff with Family Christian Stores for the past twenty-three years. He is currently the Senior Buyer of Book, Bibles, and Church Resources. Tim and his wife, Ramona, live in Grand Rapids, Michigan. They have three grown children and three grandchildren.

Dr. Criswell Freeman is a best-selling author with over 14,000,000 books in print. He is a graduate of Vanderbilt University. He received his doctoral degree from the Adler School of Professional Psychology in Chicago; he also attended classes at Southern Seminary in Louisville where he was mentored by the late Wayne Oates, a pioneer in the field of pastoral counseling. Dr. Freeman is married; he has two children.